A Narrow Gauge View of North Wales (1955-88)

Terry Gough ARPS

©Kestrel Railway Books and Terry Gough 2009

Kestrel Railway Books
PO Box 269
SOUTHAMPTON
SO30 4XR

www.kestrelrailwaybooks.co.uk

All rights reserved.

No part of this publication may be
reproduced, stored in a retrieval system,
transmitted in any form or by any means,
electronic, mechanical, or photocopied,
recorded or otherwise, without the
consent of the publisher in writing.

Printed by The Amadeus Press

ISBN 978-1-905505-14-2

Front cover: An evening train on the Ffestiniog Railway drifts over The Cob toward Porthmadog in 1980.

Back cover, top: The lower slopes of Snowdon, with a train from the Summit descending to Llanberis in September 1979.

Back cover, bottom: A typical Ffestiniog Railway train with beautifully clean engine and coaches, nears the end of its journey in Spring 1980.

Title page: Talyllyn Railway locomotive "Dolgoch" (No 2) at Pendre engine shed, being prepared for a day's work in 1988.

A Narrow Gauge View of North Wales (1955-88)

Terry Gough ARPS

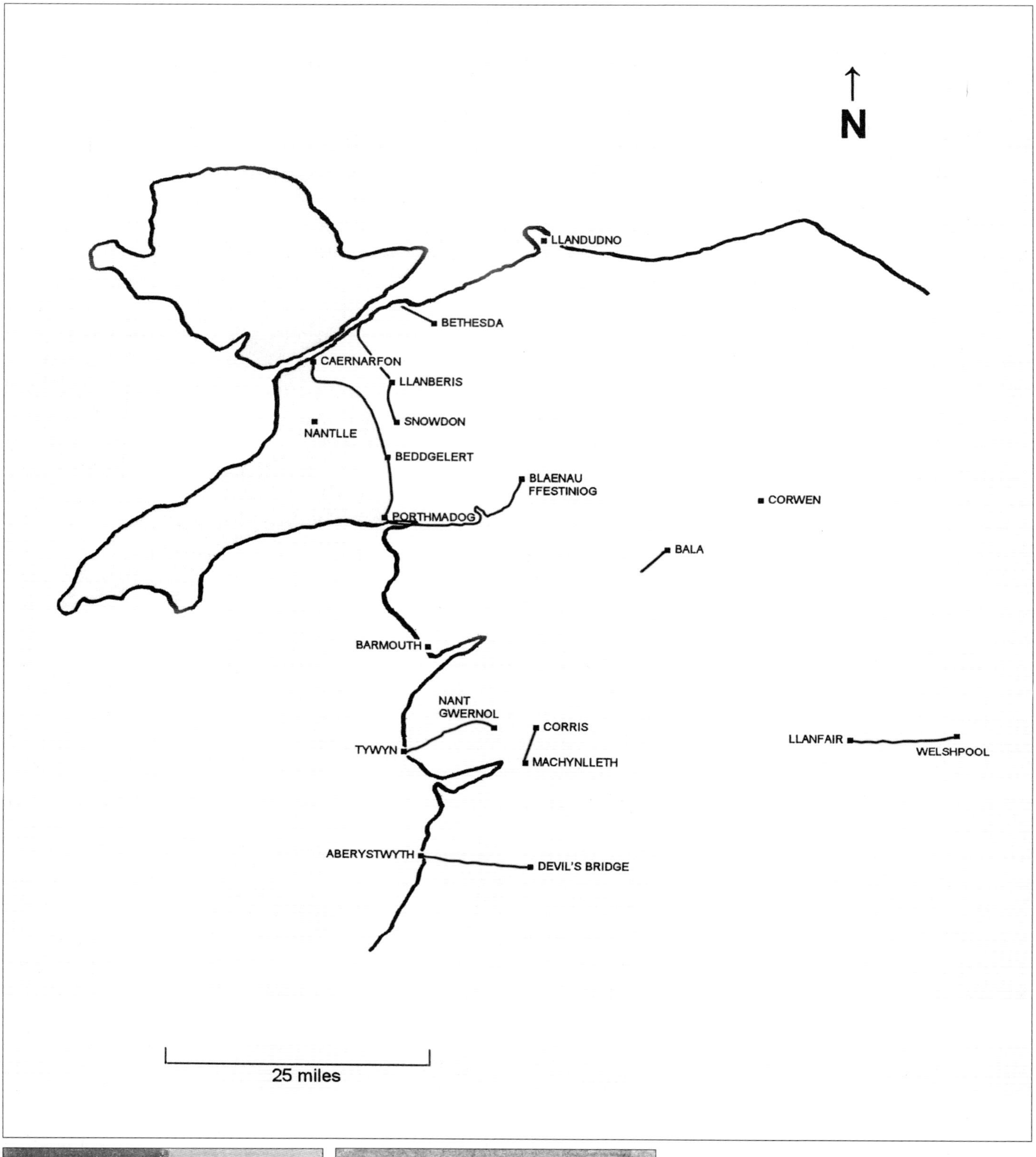

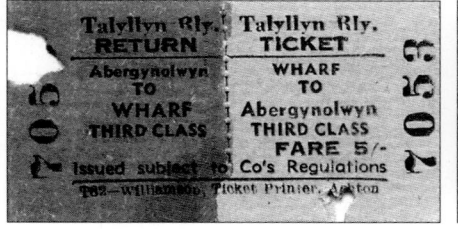 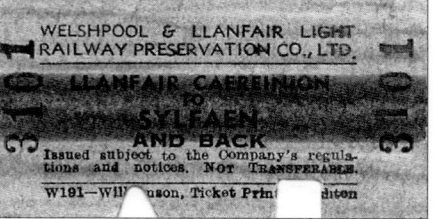 *Two tickets from 1972. The 3rd class Talyllyn Railway ticket (far left) is coloured pink and light green, and the Welshpool & Llanfair Railway ticket has a purple stripe on a turquoise background.*

Contents

Acknowledgements v

Abbreviations v

Bibliography vi

Introduction 1

Penrhyn Railway 3

Dinorwic Quarries and Llanberis Lake Railway 13

Snowdon Mountain Railway 22

Welsh Highland Railway 35

Ffestiniog Railway 47

Bala Lake Railway 68

Talyllyn Railway 73

Corris Railway 90

Welshpool & Llanfair Light Railway 96

Vale of Rheidol Railway 110

Index 127

Acknowledgements

I thank the various railway and quarrying companies who willingly gave me permission to enter areas not normally accessible to the public, or provided information. I especially thank John Bate and John Smallwood (Talyllyn Railway), Richard Greenhough (Corris Railway Society), Roger Hine (Bala Lake Railway), David Jones (Llanberis Lake Railway), John Wooden (Ffestiniog and Welsh Highland Railways), the staff of the Snowdon Mountain Railway (in particular Jonathan Tyler) and the Welshpool & Llanfair Light Railway. I record my appreciation to the young lady named Cynthia who accompanied me on many of the trips, initially believing that visits were entirely to admire the natural beauty of North Wales. Abandoned railways and piles of slate were a bonus. Although no engine has ever been named after her, she still enjoys our periodic visits to the revitalised narrow gauge railways.

Abbreviations

BR	British Railways
DMU	Diesel Multiple Unit
GWR	Great Western Railway
LMSR	London, Midland & Scottish Railway
LNWR	London & North Western Railway
RAF	Royal Air Force
VR	Vale of Rheidol Railway
WHR	Welsh Highland Railway
WLLR	Welshpool & Llanfair Light Railway

Bibliography

General

Boyd, JIC, *Narrow Gauge Railways in Mid-Wales* (Oakwood Press, 1970) ISBN 0853610835

Boyd, JIC, *Narrow Gauge Railways in North Caernarvonshire Volume 1* (Oakwood Press, 1981) ISBN 0853612730

Boyd, JIC, *Narrow Gauge Railways in South Caernarvonshire Volume 1* (Oakwood Press, 1988) ISBN 0853613656

Johnson, Peter, *The Welsh Narrow Gauge Railways* (Ian Allan, 1985) ISBN 0711014949

Johnson, Peter, *Welsh Narrow Gauge, A view from the Past* (Ian Allan, 1999) ISBN 0711026548

Kidner, RW, *The Narrow Gauge Railways of North Wales* (Oakwood Press, 1937)

Middlemass, Thomas, *Encyclopaedia of Narrow Gauge Railways of Great Britain and Ireland* (Guild Publishing, 1991)

Neal, Andrew, *Welsh Narrow Gauge Railways from Old Picture Postcards* (Plateway Press, 1991) ISBN 1871980089

Peters, Ivo, *The Narrow Gauge Charm of Yesterday* (OPC, 1976) ISBN 090288865X

Roberts, Jim, *North Wales Transport* (Sutton, 1998) ISBN 0750917229

Thomas, Cliff, *Quarry Hunslets of North Wales* (Oakwood Press, 2001) ISBN 0853615756

Welsh Mountain Railways, Great Western Railway Guide 1924 (Corris and Talyllyn Railways Societies, 1985) ISBN 9780950585802

Whitehouse, PB, *Welsh Narrow Gauge Album* (Ian Allan, 1969) ISBN 711000816

Whitehouse, PB and Snell, JB, *Narrow Gauge Railways of the British Isles* (David & Charles, 1984) ISBN 0715385232

Penrhyn Railway

Boyd, JIC, *Narrow Gauge Railways in North Caernarvonshire Volume 2* (Oakwood Press, 1985) ISBN 0853613125

Lee, Charles E, *The Penrhyn Railway* (Welsh Highland Light Railway, 1972)

Llanberis Lake Railway

Boyd, JIC, *Narrow Gauge Railways in North Caernarvonshire Volume 3* (Oakwood Press, 1986) ISBN 0853613281

Carrington, Douglas C, *Slates to Velinheli* (Bala Lake Railway Society, 1993) ISBN 095129704

Llanberis Railway Guide Book (undated)

Padarn Lake Railway Souvenir Guide Book (1983)

Snowdon Mountain Railway

Jones, Norman, *Snowdon Mountain Railway, Llanberis* (Foxline, 1997) ISBN 1870119509

Morris, OJ, *The Snowdon Mountain Railway* (Ian Allan, 1960)

Ransome-Wallis, P, *Snowdon Mountain Railway* (Ian Allan, 1969) ISBN 711001103

Turner, Keith, *The Snowdon Mountain Railway* (David & Charles, 1973) ISBN 0715358758

Turner, Keith, *The Way to the Stars* (Gwasg Carreg Gwalch, 2005) ISBN 0863819540

BIBLIOGRAPHY

Ffestiniog and Welsh Highland Railways

Bailey, Trevor, *Festiniog Railway Guide Book* (Ian Allan, 1963)

Boyd, JIC, *The Festiniog Railway* (Oakwood Press):
    Volume 1 (2002) ISBN 085361167X
    Volume 2 (2002) ISBN 0853611688

Boyd, JIC, *Narrow Gauge Railways in South Caernarvonshire Volume 2* (Oakwood Press, 1989) ISBN 0853613 834

Festiniog Railway Guide Book (1959)

Festiniog Railway Companion (1973)

More About the Welsh Highland Railway (David & Charles, 1972) ISBN 0715347675

Ingham, Paul, Johnson, Peter, Rees, Paul and Weaver, Rodney, *Festiniog Railway Locomotives* (AB Publishing, 1988) ISBN 1869915038

Johnson, Peter, *Festiniog 150th Anniversary: A Celebration* (AB Publishing, 1987) ISBN 1866915011

Johnson, Peter, *Festiniog 150: The History of the Festiniog Railway* (Ian Allan, 1987) ISBN 0711016585

Johnson, Peter, *An Illustrated History of the Welsh Highland Railway* (OPC, 2009) ISBN 9780860936268

Johnson, Peter, *Portrait of the Welsh Highland Railway* (Ian Allan, 1999) ISBN 0711026580

Lee, Charles E, *The Welsh Highland Railway* (David & Charles, 1962)

Mitchell, Vic and Smith, Keith, *Branch Lines around Porthmadog 1954-94* (Middleton Press, 1994) ISBN 1873793312

Mitchell, Vic, Smith, Keith, Gray, Adrian and Seymour, Michael, *Branch Lines around Portmadoc 1923-46* (Middleton Press, 1993) ISBN 1873793138

Shear, Bryan, *The Welsh Highland Railway; A Pictorial Guide* (Welsh Highland Light Railway [1964] Ltd, 1983)

Stretton, M John, *Ffestiniog in Camera* (Challenger, 1999) ISBN 1899624406

Stretton, John, *The Ffestiniog Railway* (Silver Link Publishing, 1998) ISBN 1858951410

Stretton, John, *The Ffestiniog and Welsh Highland Railways* (Silver Link Publishing, 1996) ISBN 1858950910

Stretton, John, *The Welsh Highland Railway* (Silver Link Publishing, 1999) ISBN 1858951429

Stretton, John, *The Welsh Highland Railway Volume 2* (Silver Link Publishing, 2004) ISBN 1858952336

Stretton, John, *The Welsh Highland Railway Volume 3* (Silver Link Publishing, 2009) ISBN 9781858952598

A Traveller's Guide (Ffestiniog Railway Company, 1972) ISBN 978090184031

Welsh Highland Railway Guide Book and Stock List (Welsh Highland Light Railway [1964] Ltd, 1983)

Bala Lake Railway

A Visitor's Guide to the Bala Lake Railway (Bala Lake Railway Society, 1985)

Talyllyn Railway

Boyd JIC, *The Talyllyn Railway* (Wild Swan, 1988) ISBN 0906867460

Cozens, Lewis, *Talyllyn Railway* (Talyllyn Railway Preservation Society, 1977) ISBN 0900317043

Mitchell, David J and Eyres, Terry, *The Talyllyn Railway* (Silver Link, 1996) ISBN 1858951259

Rolt, LTC, *Railway Adventure* (David & Charles, 1977)

Rolt, LTC, *Talyllyn Century* (David & Charles, 1965)

Stretton, John, *The Talyllyn Railway* (Silver Link Publishing, 1996) ISBN 1858951259

Talyllyn Handbook (David & Charles, 1969)

Talyllyn Railway Official Guide (Talyllyn Railway Preservation Society, 1953)

Talyllyn Railway Walks (Welsh Book Council, 2004) ISBN 8888039090

White, Christopher, *Talyllyn Railway Extension* (Talyllyn Railway Preservation Society, 1978) ISBN 090031706X

Corris Railway

Briwnant-Jones, G, *Great Western Corris* (Gomer, 1994) ISBN 1859020798

Briwnant-Jones, G, *The Last Days of the Old Corris* (Gomer, 2001) ISBN 1843230119

The Corris Railway Guide of 1895 (Corris Railway Society reprint)

Cozens, Lewis, *The Corris Railway 1949* (Corris Railway Society reprint, 1992)

Morgan, John Scott, *Corris, A Narrow Gauge Portrait* (Irwell Press, 1991) ISBN 187160818X

A Return to Corris (Avon-Anglia, 1988) ISBN 0905466896

Welshpool & Llanfair Light Railway

Ballantyne, Hugh, *The Welshpool & Llanfair Light Railway* (Silver Link Publishing, 2000) ISBN 1858951569

Cartwright, R and Russell, RT, *The Welshpool & Llanfair Light Railway* (David & Charles, 1989) ISBN 0715392263

Cozens, Lewis, *Welshpool & Llanfair Light Railway* (Cozens, 1951)

Wakeman, Michael, *Welshpool & Llanfair Light Railway* (Welshpool & Llanfair Light Railway Preservation Co, 1963)

The Welshpool & Llanfair Light Railway Illustrated Guide (1986) ISBN 0905929020

Vale of Rheidol Railway

Ballantyne, Hugh, *The Vale of Rheidol Railway* (Silver Link Publishing, 2003) ISBN 1858951550

Davies, WJK, *Vale of Rheidol Light Railway* (Ian Allan, 1978) ISBN 71100143X

Green, CC, *Rheidol Journey* (Green, 1984) ISBN 0950664219

Green, CC, *Vale of Rheidol Light Railway* (Wild Swan, 1986) ISBN 0906867436

Troughton, William, *Aberystwyth & District and the Vale of Rheidol* (SB, 1991) ISBN 1857700031

Young, Norman R, *What You Will See in the Vale of Rheidol* (West Wales Naturalist's Trust, 1971) ISBN 0902794019

Introduction

Most of the narrow gauge railways in North Wales were built primarily to transport slate within the quarries and to ports for transhipment to other parts of the UK and overseas. A few were built for the carriage of general merchandise and passengers. Two were built for tourists, a function that all the surviving lines now perform. Even on my first visit to North Wales, only two railways were transporting slate, and even these were to close within a few years. Despite the ugly landscape resulting from quarrying, it was impressive to view a quarry from the surrounding hillside. There was such activity, with tiny puffs of smoke signifying an ancient engine hauling a few wagons laden with recently-blasted slate.

I first heard of the existence of narrow gauge railways in Wales through an article on the virtually defunct Ffestiniog Railway in a late 1940s edition of *The Meccano Magazine*. In the last paragraph, the author (EV Clayton) states, "When I visited the Portmadoc terminal station the paint was peeling from signals and buildings and from the toy-like vans and wagons standing in the grass-grown sidings". A few years later, I heard that the Talyllyn Railway was about to be taken over by what was called a preservation society. I had noted from my 1947 edition of *ABC of GWR Locomotives* that against seven were asterisks, which to my surprise indicated narrow gauge. It was time to see these railways for myself. Distance and hence cost was a major barrier, so I decided to cycle. I left home in Surrey on 3rd August 1954, and reached Aberystwyth eight days later, whereupon I took my first trip on a narrow gauge railway, to Devil's Bridge and back. I continued north to Machynlleth, where I traced the route of the closed Corris Railway, then over the mountain to Talyllyn to see another active railway, very different in character to the Vale of Rheidol line. I continued to Porthmadog, but there was little activity on the Ffestiniog Railway, so I went on to Llanberis and thence to Snowdon Summit. I had to walk, as the train fare was beyond my meagre pocket. My final stop for narrow gauge lines was at Welshpool, which was on the point of closure. The trip took sixteen days in all, during which I travelled sixteen miles by train and 784 miles by bicycle. I took very few photographs, but came back with some wonderful memories and the desire to return to North Wales. This I did two years later, again by bicycle, but this time in an anticlockwise direction. The Welshpool & Llanfair line had closed, and the cost of a trip up Snowdon was still too expensive for me. I visited the Aberglaslyn Pass, and walked along the trackbed of the Welsh Highland Railway. The Corris Railway looked as though it had gone forever, and the feeling of despondency was made worse by appalling weather. I spent a night in the old engine shed at Maespoeth. I endeavoured to sleep on a workbench, but it was excruciatingly uncomfortable, made worse by rainwater pouring through the roof. To see the reawakening of the Ffestiniog Railway was the reward for all this effort, as there was an embryonic service, which was running from Porthmadog to Boston Lodge.

In 1959 I made the journey by steam train, using the "Cambrian Coast Express" from Paddington to Porthmadog. At last, I was able to make the trip up Snowdon by train. I then walked down the Snowdon Ranger path, regretting that I was twenty-two years too late for the last train on the Welsh Highland Railway, as I needed to return to Porthmadog. The possibility of this ever being rebuilt seemed even less than for the Corris Railway. The Ffestiniog Railway had reached Tan-y-bwlch, and the ride was amazing. There were superb views of the Vale of Ffestiniog, something which in later years became lost because of aforestation. Trips were also taken on the Talyllyn Railway and along the Vale of Rheidol. The return journey to London was from Barmouth via Corwen.

I visited the Penrhyn Railway in 1960 and saw a thriving system. My second visit five years later found a railway in its last days, with only a few engines operating within the quarries and nothing to Port Penrhyn. I did not visit Dinorwic Quarries until just after they had closed, and was able to see the redundant works just as they had been left on the final day of operations – a fascinating collection of Victorian machinery.

My last visit by train was behind a DMU from Shrewsbury to Aberystwyth, and then along the coast to Porthmadog. I have since made numerous visits by car, wherever possible using local standard and narrow gauge services. On one such visit to the Vale of Rheidol Railway, I endeavoured to turn the car on a narrow level crossing, but the rear wheels dropped between the sleepers. There was an urgency to resolve this problem, as I could hear the train pounding up the valley.

Since my early visits, there have been amazing transformations on several of the lines. It was not many years before the Ffestiniog Railway reached Blaenau Ffestiniog, the Talyllyn Railway extension was opened, the Welshpool & Llanfair Light Railway reopened in stages, and the future of the Vale of Rheidol Railway became more certain. The abandoned trackbed of the Welsh Highland Railway in the Aberglaslyn Pass never changed, that is until the present century, when the footpath was upgraded. Much greater change is taking place, with the rebirth of the railway over its entire length. From 2009 trains are once again passing through the tunnels of the Pass. On the Corris Railway I have seen relaid track, renovated buildings and even trains running again.

Apart from the introduction of diesel locomotives and infrastructure improvements, the Snowdon Mountain Railway has seen little change. Until the recent building of new facilities at the summit, Snowdon itself saw no change other than in the weather, which is both unpredictable and at times dramatic.

In place of the Dinorwic Quarries railway system, the Llanberis Lake Railway gives the visitor a peaceful ride along Padarn Lakeside, with excellent views of Snowdon. Much of the old quarry machinery and several of the buildings now form an excellent museum. It seems ironical that the Barmouth to Corwen main line has closed and a narrow gauge railway runs in its place along the side of Bala Lake. There are more miles of operating narrow gauge lines in the twenty first century than there were in the previous one.

I have not covered all the narrow gauge railways in North Wales. There are several others, mostly closed, although a museum of the Glyn Valley Tramway is being established. There are, however, two that are still very much operational, and which I commend to the reader. These are the Great Orme Tramway, which is cable operated, and the Fairbourne Railway, which is a miniature railway. There are also functioning narrow gauge railways further south, in particular the Teifi Valley Railway and the Brecon Mountain Railway.

All the photographs are my own, and cover the period between the mid-1950s and the 1980s. The reader is encouraged to visit North Wales to see the further changes that have taken place since this period.

I have used current spellings of place names, except where previous anglicised spellings have been used in the documents to which I am referring.

Below: A pre-1923 leaflet advertising the Festiniog Railway.

Right: A modern (1987) publicity leaflet, advertising the Cambrian Coast line of BR and the Talyllyn Railway.

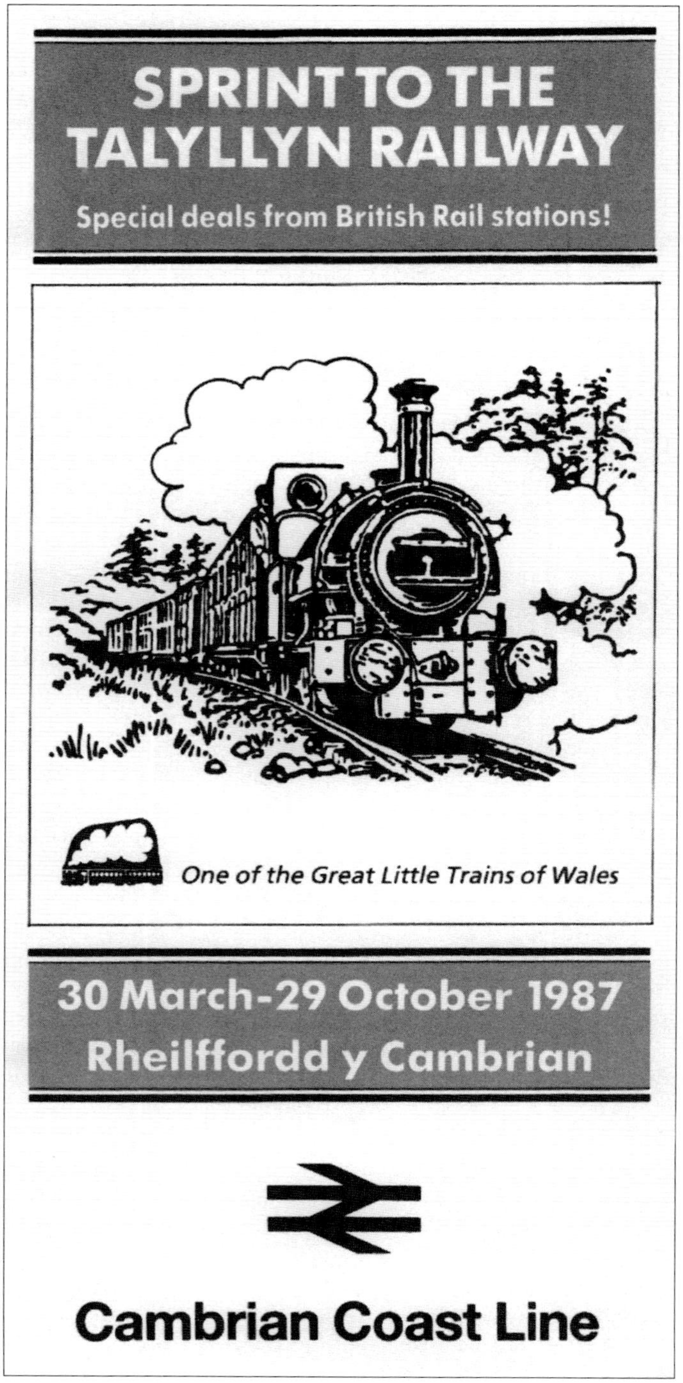

Penrhyn Railway

The Penrhyn Quarries are situated at Bethesda on the A5 trunk road south east of Bangor. Quarrying has been undertaken here for centuries with slate transported to the coast by horse, not replaced by the steam engine until 1876. There was also an extensive railway system within the quarries, with approximately 50 miles of line. Different sources quote the gauge as 1ft 10¾in, 1ft 11in and 2ft 0in. The railway survived with its fleet of ancient locomotives until 1963, when the line to Port Penrhyn was closed. The railway within the quarries closed in 1965. The course of the line to the port is still visible for much of its length. The quarries themselves are still operational, with all slate transported by road.

Above: A vast operation with mills, storage sheds, workshops and offices, all interconnected by rail. This was known as the Red Lion Level, seen in 1960. Access from here to other levels for workmen was by open carriage, hauled up the inclines by rope.

Left: Despite increased mechanisation, the traditional method of slate splitting was still used.

Views from the upper galleries give a good indication of the depth of the quarries, and also hint at the logistical problems of transferring slate to ground level and the disposal of huge amounts of waste.

"Marchlyn" was one of the more modern engines owned by the Penrhyn Railway and worked high above Bethesda. It was built in 1933, and purchased secondhand in 1936. It was in use right up to closure of the railway, when it was exported to the USA. The three-sided wagons were used for carrying waste from the quarry working face to the tip. The wheels had flanges on both the inner and outer faces. The 'LS' painted on the second wagon in front of the engine refers to the left (ie, east) side incline. Failure to observe 'left' or 'right' could result in the wagon emptying its load on the incline.

"Marchlyn". Engines were allocated to specific levels. This engine spent much of its life on the Twlldyndwr Level.

"Cegin" was built in 1931, and unlike "Marchlyn", has well tanks. This gives it a peculiarly delicate, but not particularly attractive appearance. It was also exported to the USA. Even in the 1960s, all slate wagons originated from the late nineteenth century, although much rebuilt.

"Winifred" was one of the traditional quarry engines, being built in 1885 and purchased new. The open cab gives it a really old fashioned appearance, and the crew no doubt found the lack of protection uncomfortable in bad weather. The letters 'PM' on the runner are thought to refer to the engine's allocation to the Princess May Level. This is yet another of the Penrhyn engines that went to the USA.

Above: "Blanche" was used exclusively on the line to Port Penrhyn and is seen here arriving at Coed-y-parc Yard with a train of slate wagons. The third vehicle is a brake van, converted in 1956 from the steam locomotive named "Sandford".

Left: Later the same day "Blanche" is preparing its train of finished slate for transfer to the Port. "Blanche" and its sister engine "Linda" were built in 1893. They were named after the wife and daughter of a member of the Quarry owning family. Both engines survive, and can be seen at work on the Ffestiniog Railway. A third identical engine ("Charles") is in the Penrhyn Castle Museum.

A NARROW GAUGE VIEW OF NORTH WALES (1955-88)

Left: In the years leading up to closure, an increasing number of engines were taken out of service and dumped. "Stanhope", along with several other engines, remained in this location for at least five years, before being cannibalised for spares for similar engines.

Below: "Sgt Murphy", an austere looking engine, was purchased in 1921. It was acquired by the Conwy Valley Railway Museum in 1964.

PENRHYN RAILWAY

Above: The odd looking engine in the front with the vertical boiler was one of several built in 1876/77 for the Penrhyn Railway. Most were withdrawn in the early 1900s as more conventional engines were purchased. Two survive, "George Henry", which went to the Narrow Gauge Railway Museum at Tywyn Wharf station in 1955, and "Kathleen", which went to Aberystwyth. The saddle tank is "Jubilee 1897", which is also at Tywyn.

Left: The leading engine is "Eigiau", which was built in Germany in 1912. It was named after a lake in the Conwy Valley where it was used at an aluminium factory until purchased by Penrhyn Quarries in 1928. It is currently located in Kent on the Bredgar & Wormshill Light Railway.

A NARROW GAUGE VIEW OF NORTH WALES (1955-88)

Left: In the front of the line in 1965 is "Lilian", which had not been used since 1956. The second engine is "Edward Sholto", named after an owner of the quarries, and is another traditional open cab quarry engine, which was built in 1909. Disposal was not, as expected, to a scrap merchant, but to a museum in Canada. Beyond "Edward Sholto" are "Lilla" and "Jubilee 1897". "Lilla" survived to be sold in 1963 and spent many years in Surrey. It went to the Bala Lake Railway in 1992 and subsequently to the Ffestiniog Railway.

Below: "Lilian" was not scrapped and together with "Covertcoat" (from the Padarn Railway) was transferred to Cornwall for use on the Launceston Steam Railway.

Dinorwic Quarries and the Llanberis Lake Railway

The Padarn Railway introduced steam engines in 1848 to convey slate from Llanberis to Port Dinorwic. This was a 4ft 0in gauge line, although in the quarries themselves, the gauge was 1ft 10¾in. There were several engines that worked the line to the port, one of which is now in Penrhyn Castle Museum. A quarryman's train ran until 1947, and the railway continued to transport slate until 1961. The railway within the quarries operated almost until the quarries closed in 1969. Thus was born the Llanberis Lake Railway, which is entirely for the benefit of tourists. It runs along the trackbed of the line to the port, but to a gauge of 1ft 11½in, and not the original 4ft 0in. The first passenger trains ran during the summer of 1971 from the main works at Gilfach Ddu for about a mile along the side of Llyn Padarn. The works themselves now form the Welsh Slate Museum. The line was extended further along the Lake to Penllyn for the next season. The only intermediate station is Cei Llydan. In 2003, the line was extended in the other direction to a point almost opposite the Snowdon Mountain Railway's Llanberis station. Trains run between February and December, in busy periods, with two in the morning and every half hour in the afternoon. The return trip takes about one hour.

Dinorwic Quarries in 1959, ten years prior to closure. On the left is the Snowdon Mountain Railway station of Llanberis, and running left to right across the photograph is the Caernarfon to Capel Curig road. Gilfach Ddu is on the far left near the foot of the mountain.

Above: A distant view across Llyn Padarn of a train from Gilfach Ddu en route to Port Dinorwic in July 1959. The engine is one of two built in the 1880s. Neither of these, nor an identical engine purchased in 1895 survive, all three having been cut up in 1963.

Opposite page: Four of the narrow gauge steam engines were still in serviceable condition at Dinorwic Quarries at closure. One of these was "Elidir", still in use today on the Llanberis Lake Railway.

Above: "Elidir" was built in 1889 and initially named "Enid". It was subsequently renamed "Red Damsel" after a racehorse, which seems particularly unsuitable for such an engine. In 1970 it was renamed again, this time after the mountain on which are situated the Dinorwic Quarries. "Elidir" was a popular name, as it was also carried by a 1933 built engine and by a ship operated by Dinorwic Quarries.

Opposite page: The majority of the engines survived closure of the quarries, and can be seen at various locations in the UK (for example see page 12) and Canada. In addition to "Elidir", two others can be seen on the Llanberis Lake Railway. These are "Dolbadarn" and "Thomas Bach" (formerly named "Wild Aster"). The photograph shows "Una" in the engine shed at Gilfach Ddu. It is owned by the Museum, but is available for use on the railway. It was built in 1905 and came from the Pen-yr-orsedd Quarries at Nantlle.

A NARROW GAUGE VIEW OF NORTH WALES (1955-88)

DINORWIC QUARRIES AND THE LLANBERIS LAKE RAILWAY

The first wagon is for carrying slabs of slate. The covered vehicle is a gunpowder van of the type used at the Oakeley Quarries at Blaenau Ffestiniog (see pages 64 and 65). Smaller slates were stacked vertically in frame-sided wagons, seen behind the gunpowder van.

Opposite page top: Part of the abandoned quarry railway system. There is a footpath, open to the public, through one of the quarries. This forms part of the Padarn Country Park, which also incorporates a nature trail.

Opposite page bottom: An assortment of open wagons and a brake van on the rear. Trains of finished slate, which ran from Gilfach Ddu to Port Dinorwic, consisted of 4ft gauge transporter wagons, each loaded with four narrow gauge slate wagons. Examples of these wagons can be seen at the Narrow Gauge Railway Museum in Tywyn.

A NARROW GAUGE VIEW OF NORTH WALES (1955-88)

Above: The clue to new life for "Dolbadarn" lies to the right of the engine, where a passenger coach can be seen. The engine is taking water at Gilfach Ddu after a trip along the lakeside in 1988.

Right: This is the same engine later in the day with its train on the lakeside. Unlike the goods stock, the passenger coaches are all modern, being built in the 1970s. They are all bogie vehicles and have doors on one side only.

DINORWIC QUARRIES AND THE LLANBERIS LAKE RAILWAY

Above: There is no station at the terminus of Penllyn, but passengers can alight at Cei Llydan. "Dolbadarn" is seen here on its return journey to Gilfach Ddu. "Dolbadarn" was used at Port Dinorwic until 1935, when it was transferred to work within the Quarries until their closure.

Right: In the height of the season two engines are in use and trains pass at Cei Llydan. This is "Elidir" on such a train.

Snowdon Mountain Railway

The desire to build railway lines up the sides of mountains is not restricted to Switzerland. There is one rack railway in the UK, and this ascends Snowdon. Metrication arrived early in Wales, as the Snowdon Mountain Railway was built to a gauge of 800mm. The simple explanation is that the line was built using a rack system invented in Switzerland. The railway from Llanberis to Snowdon Summit was opened in 1896. It is 4¾ miles long, and the steepest gradient is 1 in 5½. At several points, the gradient is 1 in 6, the first of which is encountered shortly after leaving Llanberis. It initially had three Swiss-built engines, shortly followed by two more, and then another three to a similar design in the 1920s. Diesel motive power was introduced in 1988 with the purchase of two locomotives. There were intermediate stations at Waterfall, Hebron, Halfway, Rocky Valley and Clogwyn, all except the first having passing loops. Waterfall closed in the 1960s, but the others remain open. In bad weather, trains may terminate at one of these stations. Each train consists of a single coach pushed up the mountain and not coupled to the engine. Services are provided between March and October, with a frequency dependant on demand.

The engine shed and works is located at Llanberis in sight of the station. Several of the engines are named after local mountains, and in July 1959 "Moel Siabod" (No 5) and "Wyddfa" (No 3) are outside the shed.

SNOWDON MOUNTAIN RAILWAY

Right: Newly arrived diesel engine "Ninian" (No 9) is in a similar position 29 years later. The track in the centre of the photograph leads to the Summit. No 9 is named after the company chairman. The coach is also new, having been delivered only a few weeks earlier.

Below: "Enid" (No 2) is being coaled and watered in preparation for its next trip to the Summit.

A NARROW GAUGE VIEW OF NORTH WALES (1955-88)

Both pictures: "Padarn" (No 6) and "Enid", together with their coaches are on shed prior to the start of the day's service.

SNOWDON MOUNTAIN RAILWAY

Maintenance and even heavy repair work are undertaken on site. Two views of the works interior show (left) "Ralph Sadler" (No 7) and "Snowdon" (No 4). No 7, initially called "Eryri" and then "Aylwin", was later named after Ralph Sadler who was the railway's consultant engineer. This completes the steam fleet, as "Ladas" (No 1) was written off in an accident on the opening day.

A NARROW GAUGE VIEW OF NORTH WALES (1955-88)

Above: Portrait of "Moel Siabod" and "Enid". The latter is named after the daughter of a local landowner, whose estate included Snowdon and Dinorwic Quarries (see page 16).

Opposite page: Another activity prior to the start of the day is track maintenance, here being undertaken in Llanberis station.

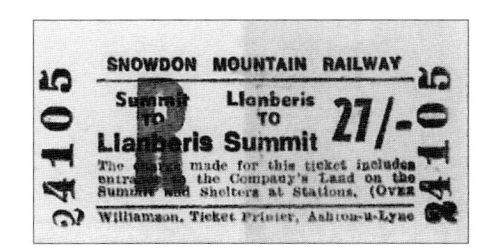

Both pictures: There is little need for non-passenger trains, but there are engineers and supplies trains, the latter usually running during the early part of the day. "Wyddfa" leaves Llanberis on one such train.

SNOWDON MOUNTAIN RAILWAY

Right: Close up of "Yeti" (No 10) shows how much more complicated is a diesel engine.

Below: The first interesting landmark after leaving Llanberis is Waterfall Viaduct. Waterfall Station was a little before the viaduct. "Wyddfa" works a train to the Summit in summer 1959.

A NARROW GAUGE VIEW OF NORTH WALES (1955-88)

Above: This is "Padarn", just beyond Hebron in 1960, on its way to the Summit. The railway initially had six coaches, followed by three more in 1922. Seven were rebuilt in the 1950s, one was scrapped and one converted into a guard's van (see opposite page).

Opposite page top: Twenty years later "Enid" works the morning supplies train near Hebron. The vehicle next to the engine was converted from one of the original coaches. In addition to the guard's compartment, there is a coal bunker and water tank, the contents of which are for the Summit facilities.

Opposite page bottom: "Moel Siabod" is seen just before Hebron on a clear day in 1979. The weather can change without warning, particularly beyond Halfway, and many passengers expecting to have a clear view from the Summit are disappointed.

A NARROW GAUGE VIEW OF NORTH WALES (1955-88)

This page and opposite page: The landscape is beginning to have a more barren look as Halfway is approached. In the second photograph both trains are ascending the mountain.

SNOWDON MOUNTAIN RAILWAY

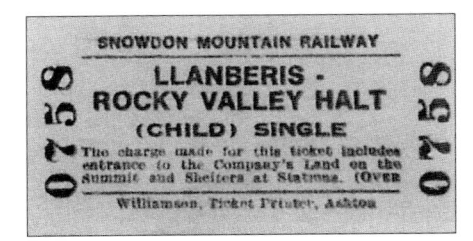

A NARROW GAUGE VIEW OF NORTH WALES (1955-88)

Left: Waiting in the passing loop at Clogwen afforded an excellent view of a descending train in 1959.

Below: This view from high on Snowdon looking north, shows Clogwen Station in the distance and a train beyond.

34

Welsh Highland Railway

The North Wales Narrow Gauge Railways ran from Dinas Junction, near Caernarfon, to Porthmadog. The line was opened as far as Quellyn, with a branch to the quarries at Bryngwyn, in 1877, and was extended south to reach Rhyd Ddu in 1881. It was built to a gauge of 1ft 11½in for the conveyance of slate, general merchandise and passengers. Further south, a tramway had been built in 1863 from Porthmadog to Croesor. It seemed obvious that by extending the line south from Rhyd Ddu, Porthmadog could be reached using part of the tramway route. Both railways were in financial difficulties, and this, combined with legal difficulties and the First World War, meant that it was not until 1922 that the two railways were taken over by the Welsh Highland (Light Railway) Company. The following year, the line linking the two railways was completed, and through passenger services between Dinas Junction and Porthmadog commenced. In theory at least, this gave a quicker route from Caernarfon to Porthmadog than offered by the LMSR and GWR; it was certainly much more attractive. In 1934, the Welsh Highland Railway was leased to the Ffestiniog Railway, but by this time both were in a very poor financial state. The anticipated growth in passenger traffic, particularly from tourists, never materialised, and the Welsh Highland Railway closed completely in 1937.

This was however, not the end. In 1964, a new company was formed with the intention of rebuilding the southern end of the line from Porthmadog to at least Beddgelert. A workshop was established at Gelert's Farm on the edge of Porthmadog, and in 1980, a short stretch of line from a new station at Porthmadog was opened.

In more recent times, and outside the period covered by this book, huge progress has been made at the northern end of the line by the Welsh Highland Railway (Caernarfon). It is expected that through trains from Caernarfon to Porthmadog will be running from 2009.

There are excellent views of Llyn Quellyn from the Snowdon Ranger path. This is 1959, and there is still plenty of evidence that the Welsh Highland Railway once passed this way. The house at the bottom left is the former Snowdon Ranger station and the course of the line from the station running roughly parallel with the Lake can also be seen.

A NARROW GAUGE VIEW OF NORTH WALES (1955-88)

Opposite page top: Following closure the line was dismantled, but a few structures were left for decades. These are the remains of the water tower at the site of Beddgelert station. Beyond the water tower is the former station building. The town is to the left at a lower elevation. From here, the line descended at 1 in 40 to reach Aberglaslyn Pass, where it followed the river, but at a higher elevation.

Left and above: In many places the trackbed became a footpath, one of the most attractive being through the Aberglaslyn Pass just south of Beddgelert. This section of the old line includes unlined tunnels.

Above and left: Some of the bridges still survived in 1988, and this is the bridge (from track and road level) between Nantmor and Hafod-y-llyn, both of which had stations. This A class road runs from Pont Aberglaslyn to Garreg and Penrhyndeudraeth (see page 57).

Left: South of Nantmor, the railway continued to descend, ultimately to cross flat terrain, which is only a little above sea level.

Below: Pont Croesor carries the B class road from Garreg over the Afon Glaslyn. The stone piers at one time also carried the railway line. There was a station on the Porthmadog side of the bridge, from where this photograph was taken.

A NARROW GAUGE VIEW OF NORTH WALES (1955-88)

Above: The line continued south west toward Porthmadog, crossing a minor road from Tremadog. This is Pen-y-mount in 1988, the terminus of the short section of reopened line. There were three trains per day in summer only, later increased to nine per day. The round trip from Porthmadog took thirty minutes. Some of the coaches were built at the railway's workshops at Gelert's Farm on the north eastern edge of Porthmadog using new bodies on second-hand wagon underframes.

Left: The remains of Portmadoc New station, opened in 1923 on the south side of the GWR line, with the remains of water tower and corrugated iron station building. Trains continued along the streets of Porthmadog to the terminus at the Ffestiniog Railway's Harbour Station. A replacement station was opened just before the crossing with the GWR line in 1929, and this became the terminus for Welsh Highland trains until closure eight years later.

Yet another Porthmadog station was built in 1978 and this is the terminus in 1988, situated alongside the standard gauge line close to Porthmadog ex-GWR station (visible in the background).

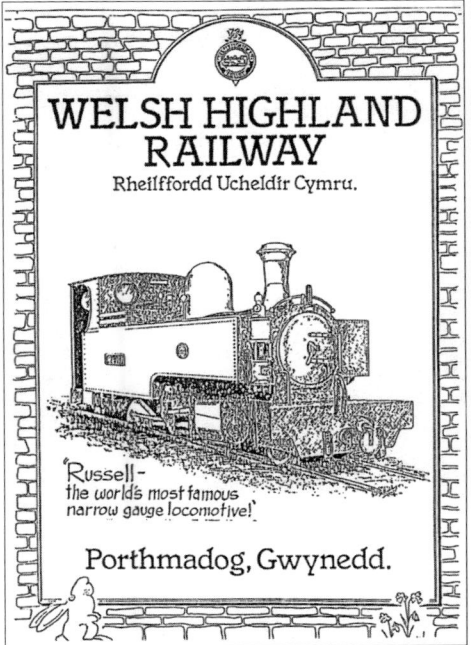

A NARROW GAUGE VIEW OF NORTH WALES (1955-88)

Top: The new railway company acquired several small diesel locomotives, which are used mainly on engineer's trains. "Glaslyn" (No 1) approaches Gelert's Farm with a train of open wagons in 1987.

Bottom: "Glaslyn" also works passenger trains and is seen on a train from Porthmadog passing Gelert's Farm Works.

"Russell" has just emerged from the shed. This engine has had an amazing survival. It was built in 1906, and used regularly between Dinas Junction and the southern terminus of the North Wales Narrow Gauge Railways. On the opening of the southern section of the line, it had to be modified in anticipation of through running to the Ffestiniog Railway. It continued to be heavily used right up to closure of the line, after which it was stored for several years. In 1942, it was sold for use in an ironstone quarry in the Midlands, and later to a clay quarrying company on the Isle of Purbeck in Dorset. In 1954 it was acquired by the Narrow Gauge Museum at Tywyn where it resided until 1965. It has since been rebuilt and restored to full running order for use on the new railway.

A NARROW GAUGE VIEW OF NORTH WALES (1955-88)

Above: Putting the finishing touches to "Russell" not long after restoration was completed in 1987.

Opposite page: Two views outside the shed at Gelert's Farm, with "Russell" and "Glaslyn".

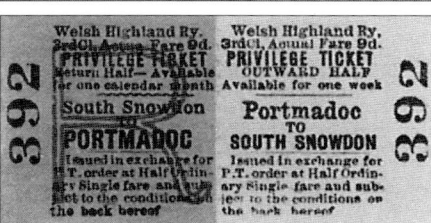

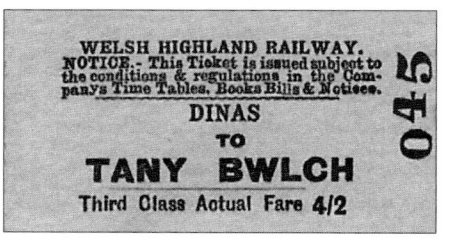

A NARROW GAUGE VIEW OF NORTH WALES (1955-88)

Top: Inside the Works is "Karen", built in 1942, and purchased by a mining company in Southern Rhodesia. It was brought to Porthmadog in 1976, rebuilt and used for the first time on the Welsh Highland Railway in 1983. The wooden bodied coach on the right was built in 1893, and the time had obviously come for it to be rebuilt. It was used regularly on the old Welsh Highland Railway, and following closure, was sold and converted into a summerhouse.

Bottom: In preparation for expansion, the railway has obtained several other locomotives, two of which are under restoration in the company's works. In the foreground is "Moel Tryfan" and behind is "Gelert". Both are post-Second World War engines, built in Stafford, and exported to South Africa for use on a mining railway.

Ffestiniog Railway

The Ffestiniog Railway was built to bring slate from the mountains around Blaenau Ffestiniog to Porthmadog for shipment. In common with the railways serving the quarries further north, horses were initially used to haul wagons. However, on the Ffestiniog Railway, loaded wagons descended from Blaenau Ffestiniog by gravity. The line was built to a gauge of 1ft 11½in. Steam traction was introduced in 1863, and two years later a passenger service was introduced on part of the line. In 1870, passenger trains were running the whole length of the line. Slate was the mainstay of the railway, and once the LNWR and GWR opened their lines to Blaenau Ffestiniog, traffic on the narrow gauge railway fell dramatically. Passenger trains ceased to run from 1939, and the railway closed completely in 1946. Passenger services were reintroduced in 1955 with trains running from Porthmadog to Boston Lodge on the other side of the estuary. Thus began an amazing change in the fortunes of the railway, extending to Minffordd a year later, then Tan-y-bwlch in 1958. Ddault was reached in 1968, Tanygrisiau a decade later, and finally Blaenau Ffestiniog in 1982. Not all the line is on the original formation, as a deviation had to be built north of Ddault because of a hydro-electric scheme. To reach the deviation, which is at a higher level than the original route, a spiral had to be built at Ddault.

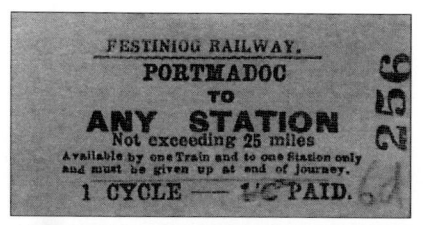

Left: Cycle ticket issued from Portmadoc to the author on 16 August 1955.

Right: Portmadoc blank Privilege of pre-Second World War style.

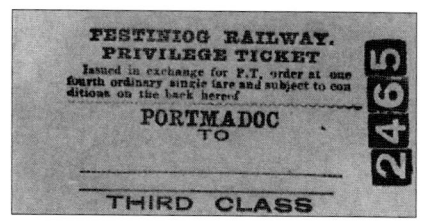

Above and overleaf top: Porthmadog Harbour Station in August 1955, with a train just arrived from Boston Lodge. Passenger services had resumed only three weeks earlier, after a gap of sixteen years. The engine is "Prince", which was built in 1863 and was the only serviceable steam engine available for the reopened railway. The leading coach is No 12, built in 1880, and rebuilt as a passenger guard's van in the 1920s, as seen here. It was rebuilt again in 1963 (see page 59). The second coach (No 23), with Third Class seating, and built in 1894, is from the Welsh Highland Railway and was obtained by the Ffestiniog Railway in 1936.

A NARROW GAUGE VIEW OF NORTH WALES (1955-88)

Left: Four years later the situation had improved a little and the more powerful "Taliesin" was in use. By this time services were running to Tan-y-bwlch, just over seven miles from Porthmadog and 430ft above sea level. It is seen here running round its train at Porthmadog in preparation for the next journey. The engine was named after the sixth century bard. In the foreground is coach No 23. To the right of the engine is one of the bow-sided composite coaches, No 18, built in 1876.

48

FFESTINIOG RAILWAY

Above: "Taliesin" continued to work on a regular basis until 1971. It is seen leaving Porthmadog in June 1960 for Tan-y-bwlch. This engine was developed for the Ffestiniog Railway from a design patented in 1864, and was built at the railway's Boston Lodge workshops in 1885. It is double-ended with a central cab, and is articulated, ideally suited to the line with its many sharp curves.

Left: With the harbourside houses of Porthmadog in the background, "Taliesin" heads across the embankment (known as The Cob) toward Boston Lodge in 1959.

A NARROW GAUGE VIEW OF NORTH WALES (1955-88)

Left: The shortage of serviceable endogenous motive power led the Ffestiniog Railway to purchase two identical engines from the then recently-closed Penrhyn Railway (see page 9). "Linda" is shunting at Porthmadog in 1965.

Bottom: An identical engine to "Prince" was "Princess", which was in use until 1946 when it hauled the last train. In the early 1960s it stood out of use at Porthmadog.

Opposite page top: In 1960, "Taliesin" passes Pen Cob Halt at the east end of The Cob on a mid-afternoon train to Tan-y-bwlch. The halt had a very short life, being opened in the spring of 1956 and closing in November 1967. The leading Third Class coach (No 26) was from the Welsh Highland Railway, and was rebuilt in 1959 (see page 67). A toll was charged for all road users crossing The Cob, the toll house being close to the halt. Tolls were not abolished until 2003.

Opposite page bottom: Sunset over The Cob as "Upnor Castle" and "Linda" return to Boston Lodge after a day's work. "Upnor Castle" was purchased in 1968 from the WLLR, which had obtained it from the Admiralty six years previously.

Below: Toll ticket issued 28th June 1959.

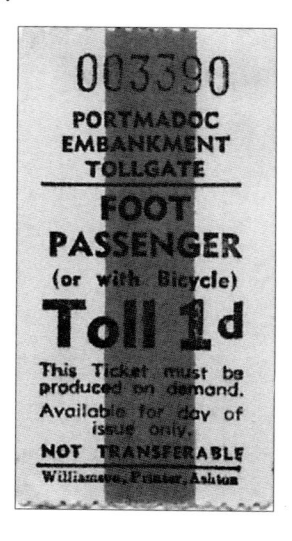

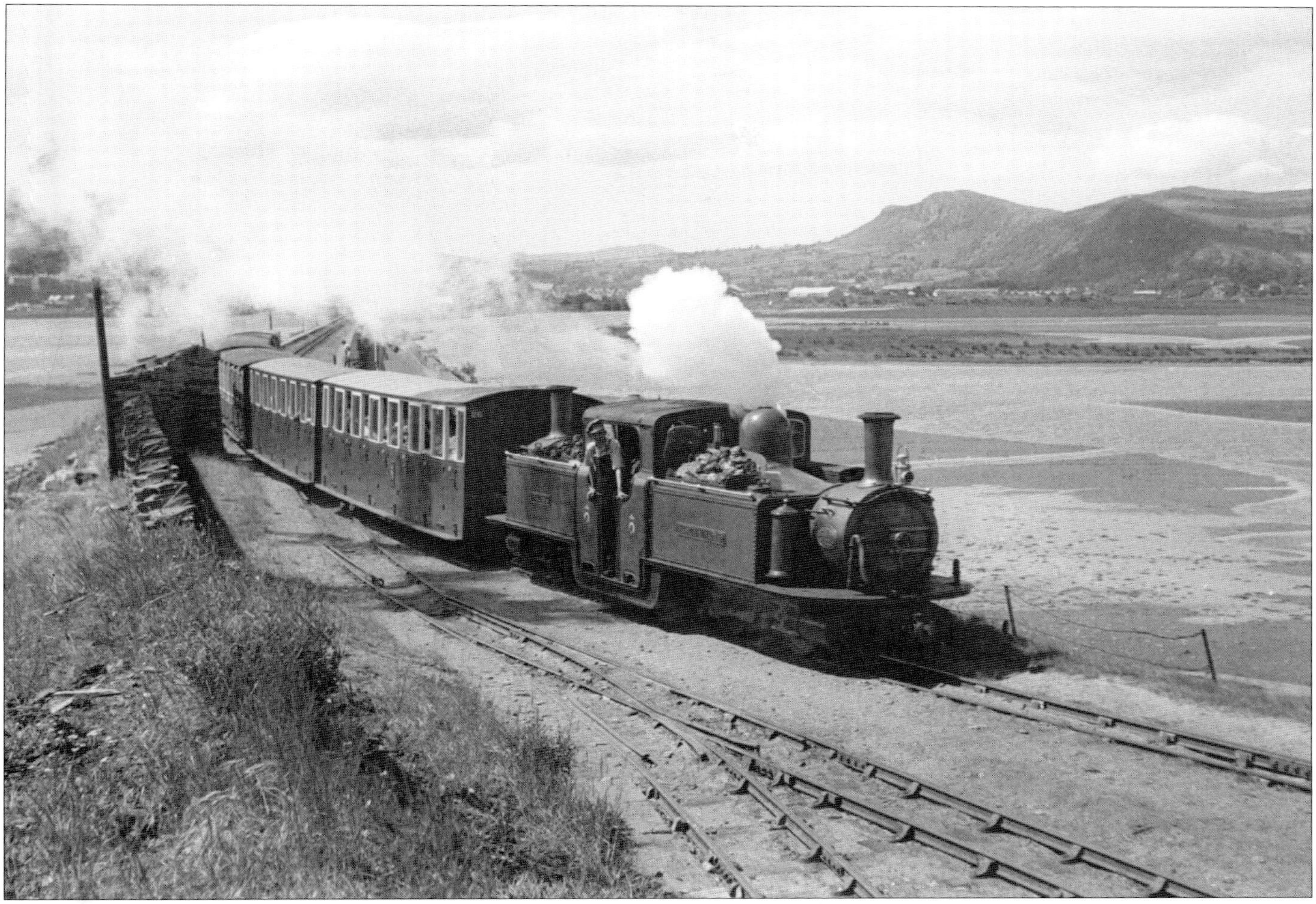

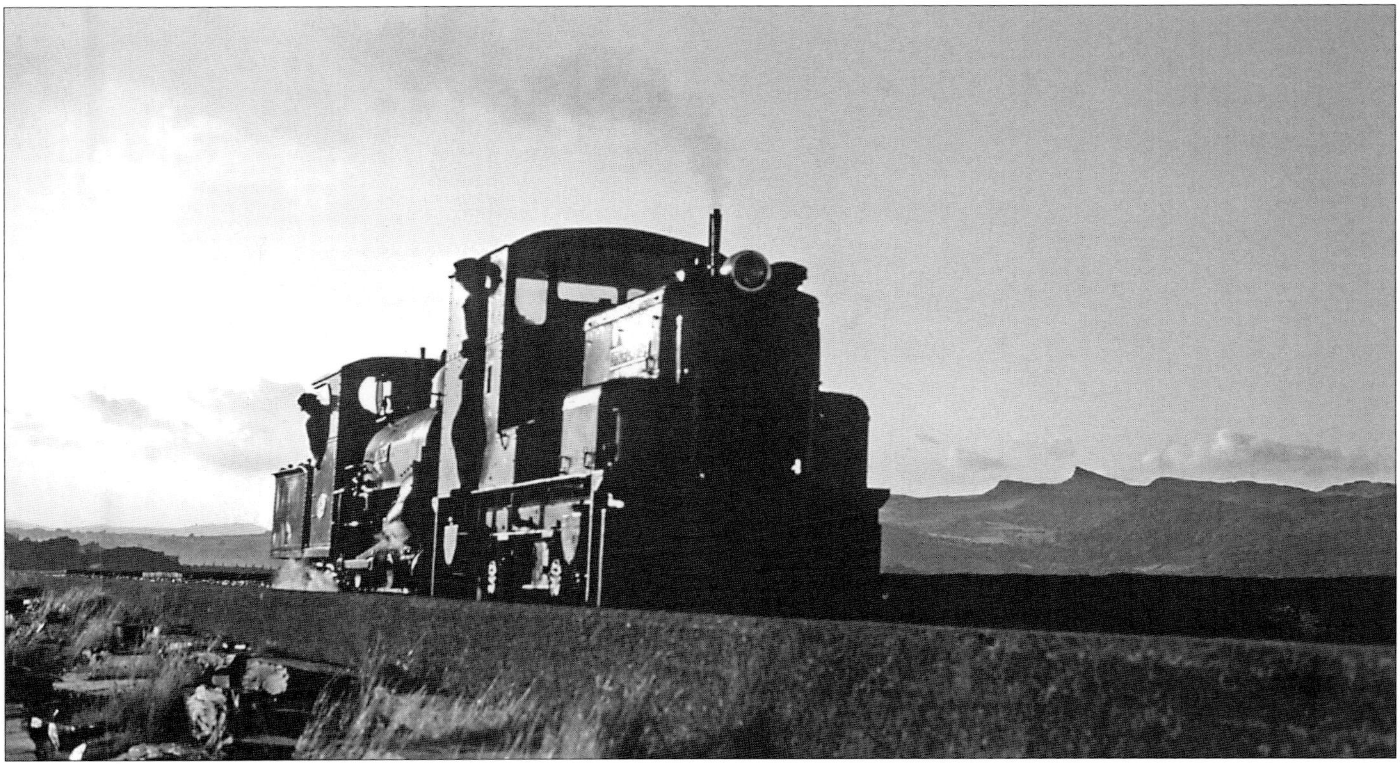

A NARROW GAUGE VIEW OF NORTH WALES (1955-88)

There are delightful views of The Cob and the mountains in the background from across Porthmadog Harbour. "Linda", one of the ex-Penrhyn Railway engines now fitted with a tender, conveys its train along the last few yards of its journey on two successive late afternoons in March 1980.

Above: Boston Lodge Works in 1955 has an air of abandonment, with locomotives and rolling stock dumped following closure of the railway nine years previously. A decrepit "Palmerston" is alongside one of the main buildings.

Right: On the same day there were more encouraging signs inside the works, with "Taliesin" undergoing major repairs. It had not been used since 1939, when it entered the Works for repairs. As the photographs on other pages show, it was ultimately restored, but only survived in an operational capacity until 1971.

By 1959 "Taliesin" had emerged from the works and was engaged in revenue earning service. The 6-wheeled coal wagon (No 8) on the right is very unusual, as it has a flexible underframe system patented by an engineer on the North Wales Narrow Gauge Railways, and built at Boston Lodge in 1878. Inset: Boston Lodge to Portmadoc (Harbour) issued 16th August 1955.

Above: "Moelwyn" is shunting a few wagons at Boston Lodge in June 1960. This locomotive was built in 1918, and its petrol engine was replaced by diesel in 1956 when it was given its name. It was of USA origin and had been in Ffestiniog Railway ownership since 1925. The brake van (No 2) had been rebuilt from a quarryman's coach of 1885, and its use is normally restricted to permanent way trains.

Right: One of the original Ffestiniog Railway engines, out of use at the back of Boston Lodge Works in 1965, and carrying the temporary name "Harold Wilson", mimicking the use of the name "Palmerston" who was Prime Minister when these engines were built.

A NARROW GAUGE VIEW OF NORTH WALES (1955-88)

Above: "Taliesin" leaves Minffordd on an afternoon train from Tan-y-bwlch to Porthmadog in 1960. The former GWR line, which runs along the coast from Aberdovey and Barmouth, passes under the Ffestiniog Railway at this point, and has its own station. A direction sign can be seen to the right of the engine.

Left: To the left of the train seen leaving Minffordd is the main road that runs from Porthmadog across The Cob and along the Vale of Ffestiniog to Maentwrog and beyond.

Below: Pram ticket from Minfford to Duffws.

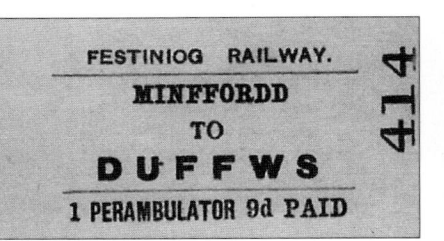

```
FESTINIOG  RAILWAY.        414
     MINFFORDD
         TO
     D U F F W S
   1 PERAMBULATOR 9d PAID
```

56

Above: Just over a mile beyond Minffordd is Penrhyndeudreath, and a train from Tan-y-bwlch approaches Penrhyn station in 1965. The engine is "Prince", next to which is an observation coach, No 100 – a new vehicle that had only been completed a matter of weeks previously. The second vehicle is a buffet car (No 14), originally a Brake Third built for the Lynton & Barnstable Railway in 1897.

Right: A few minutes later "Linda" crosses the road by the station on an up train. The road leads from Penrhyndeudreath town to Garreg (see pages 38 and 39) and the Aberglaslyn Pass.

Below: Minffordd to Blaenau Festiniog quarryman's weekly ticket.

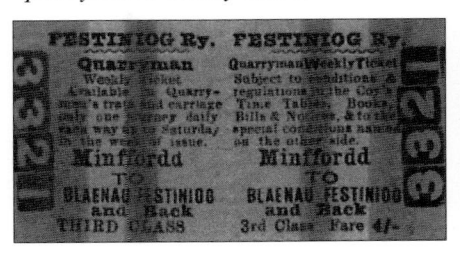

A NARROW GAUGE VIEW OF NORTH WALES (1955-88)

Above: The line was reopened as far as Penrhyn in 1957, and the loop used for running round. Initially there were seven trains per day in the height of summer. Trains often passed here when the line was extended to Tan-y-bwlch, as seen in 1971. The loop was taken out in 1981, and the platform widened. The long climb up the valley starts at Boston Lodge, continues at 1 in 86 to Minfordd, then increases to 1 in 82 through Penrhyn.

Left: The line continues to climb at 1 in 82 beyond Penrhyn, much of it in woods. It is relatively straight for about three miles, beyond which it enters a series of sharp curves. Near the first of these is Plas Halt, which was opened in 1963. In 1972 "Mountaineer" heads a train near the Halt. This is an American engine built in 1916 and was acquired by the Ffestiniog Railway in 1967.

58

Above: The line opens out at Whistling Curve, giving an excellent view of "Linda" on a down train in 1965. The leading coach is No 11, built in 1880, rebuilt at Boston Lodge in 1928 and again in 1957, on the latter occasion to a First Class observation coach. The second vehicle is No 12, now a buffet coach, but originally built in 1880 as a brake van (see page 47). Inset: Minffordd to Penrhyndeudraeth ticket.

Right: The line continues to curve sharply several times between Whistling Curve and Tan-y-bwlch, and trains will suddenly appear without visible warning, although up trains can be heard several minutes before this as they tackle the long climb.

Above: "Prince" has recently arrived at Tan-y-bwlch, and is taking water prior to the return trip to Porthmadog in 1965. Close to the station is the Snowdonia National Park Environmental Studies Centre, housed in a mansion that was at one time the property of a quarry-owning family.

Right: "Linda" arrived later in the day. It was another three years before trains could continue to Ddault. Inset: Portmadoc to Tanybwlch ticket.

FFESTINIOG RAILWAY

Above: At Creuau Bank, just beyond Tan-y-bwlch, the railway passes over a high stone embankment. "Blanche" is seen here on an up train in 1971. The leading 4-wheeled coach (No 1) was built in 1965. The second coach (No 8) is about eighty years older, rebuilt in 1962 from a quarryman's coach. The other 4-wheeled coaches (Nos 4 and 5) are even older, being built in 1863/64.

Left: This 1980 view shows trains passing at Tan-y-bwlch. On the left, "Linda" is about to leave for Porthmadog. The train on the right is continuing to Tanygrisiau, which had been reopened two years previously.

A NARROW GAUGE VIEW OF NORTH WALES (1955-88)

FFESTINIOG RAILWAY

Opposite page top: The line emerges from woods some distance beyond Tan-y-bwlch, giving good views of the trains in the vicinity of Campbell's Platform, which was opened in 1968. In 1972, "Mountaineer" descends from Ddault on a train to Porthmadog.

Opposite page bottom: "Mountaineer" is taking an up train on the main line through Ddault, while "Earl of Merioneth" waits in the loop with a train for Porthmadog on the same day. The latter is one of the locomotives that carries its name in both English and Welsh ("Iarll Meirionnydd"). It was built at Boston Lodge, and had only been completed a matter of weeks prior to this photograph being taken.

This page: "Linda" approaches Ddault on a down train in September 1979. It is at Ddault that the spiral begins in order to gain height for the new route to Tanygrisiau. Work on this deviation started in 1965, and took twelve years to complete. After leaving Ddault, the train will pass under the bridge seen on the far right of the top photograph.

63

A NARROW GAUGE VIEW OF NORTH WALES (1955-88)

The reason for the building of the Ffestiniog Railway is all the more apparent as Blaenau Ffestiniog is approached. Blaenau Ffestiniog narrow gauge exchange station was in a dilapidated state when visited in 1955. The adjacent LNWR (later LMSR) station, which was opened at the same time (1881), was the terminus of the line from Llandudno Junction. This station closed in 1982 but the line from Llandudno Junction did not close. The line had been extended in 1964 along the old Ffestiniog Railway formation to connect with the former GWR line from Bala Junction, which had lost its passenger service in 1960. This was to bring passenger services closer to the centre of Blaenau Ffestiniog, and to enable nuclear flask trains to reach Trawsfynydd from the north. A new station was opened in 1982 on the site of the old GWR terminus (Blaenau Ffestiniog Central) for BR and Ffestiniog passengers. The Ffestiniog Railway continued a short distance to its terminus, known as Duffws.

Right: Various tickets, clockwise from top-left:

Minffordd to Ddault return.

Porthmadog to Tanygrisiau paper ticket from the 1980s.

Blaenau Festiniog to Afonwen. Despite being a joint issue with the LMSR, the passenger is routed on the GWR line to Afonwen.

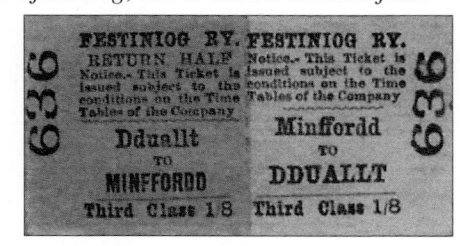

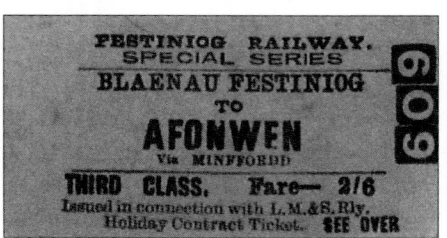

There were extensive transfer sidings close by and these were a mixture of standard and narrow gauge lines; wagons can be seen on both lines in these 1955 and 1960 views. The narrow gauge sidings were used by the quarry until 1962. The stone building is the LMSR goods shed in front of which ran the narrow gauge lines, at a higher level than the standard gauge in order to facilitate transfer of slate and other materials.

*Top: "Prince" approaches the site of the old station (see page 64) on a train from Porthmadog in July 1988.
Bottom: A train from Llandudno (DMU No T333) arrives at the new interchange station in 1988. To the right is the Ffestiniog Railway platform. A short walk from the station are the Llechwedd Slate Caverns, which are open to the public.*

Top: Shortly afterward, the Porthmadog train leaves behind "Prince". Services operate most of the year, and in the summer there are as many as ten trains per day. The journey time (one way) is just over an hour.

Bottom: The last train of the day leaves from Blaenau Ffestiniog behind "Mountaineer". The rear coach, No 26 (see page 50), was built in 1894, was rebuilt in 1959 and again in 1965. The second coach, No 118, has a very different history and was built in 1977. It is of all-metal construction with a new body mounted on an underframe from the Isle of Man Railway.

Bala Lake Railway

This line has never been associated with slate quarrying. It was built on the course of the GWR line that was closed in January 1965. It is to a gauge of 1ft 11½in, and the first section from Llanuwchllyn to Llangower was opened in 1972 for local passengers and tourists. The line was extended in 1975, and again the following year, giving a total length of 4½ miles. It runs along the lakeside to the north eastern tip of the lake to Pen-y-bont, where Bala Lake Halt (closed 1939) was once situated, just short of the site of Bala Junction. The line descends from Llanuwchllyn to the water's edge at a maximum gradient of 1 in 70. There are halts at Pentrepiod, Glanllyn (known as Flag) and Bryn Hynod, and a station with passing loop at Llangower, which is about half way. Trains operate between April and October, with three most afternoons and a morning run at peak times.

Above: The present terminus and headquarters are at the former GWR station of Llanuwchllyn, viewed from the hillside in 1988.

Left: Llanuwchllyn station looking toward Dolgellau. Both the original up and down platforms still exist, although narrow gauge track has only been laid in the former. Passenger rolling stock is all modern and purchased new by the railway. Doors are provided on one side only.

Top: This general view of Llanuwchllyn shows the shed, works and station. The shed in the foreground houses several small diesel locomotives. In the middle distance is the steam locomotive shed and the works, and beyond these are the signal box and station. The several bogie coal wagons in the yard were purchased from the RAF in 1986.

Bottom: Looking in the other direction, a train is seen arriving from Bala (Pen-y-bont). A comparison of ancient and modern, with the steam engine "Holy War" built in 1902 and "Meirionnydd", a diesel locomotive built 70 years later.

A NARROW GAUGE VIEW OF NORTH WALES (1955-88)

Above: "Holy War" spent most of its life on the Dinorwic Quarries Railway. The name was taken in 1908 from that of a racehorse, but whether this was to commemorate the Young Turk Revolution of the same year is not known – an interesting name in the context of jihad in the twenty-first century. "Holy War" was the last steam engine to work at the quarries. Following closure of the quarries, it was purchased privately and moved to the Bala Lake Railway in 1975.

Left: "Maid Marian" also came from Dinorwic Quarries. On closure of the quarries, it went initially to Norfolk and was moved to Bala in 1975.

Opposite page top: "Maid Marian" in the shed. The engine was built in 1903 and purchased new by Dinorwic Quarries.

Opposite page bottom: Inside the works are the frames of "Alice". This is another Dinorwic Quarries engine, also built in 1902. It was sold in 1972, by which time it had been dismantled to provide spares for other locomotives at the quarries. Behind "Alice" is "Chilmark", a diesel locomotive built in 1939, and purchased from the RAF establishment of that name.

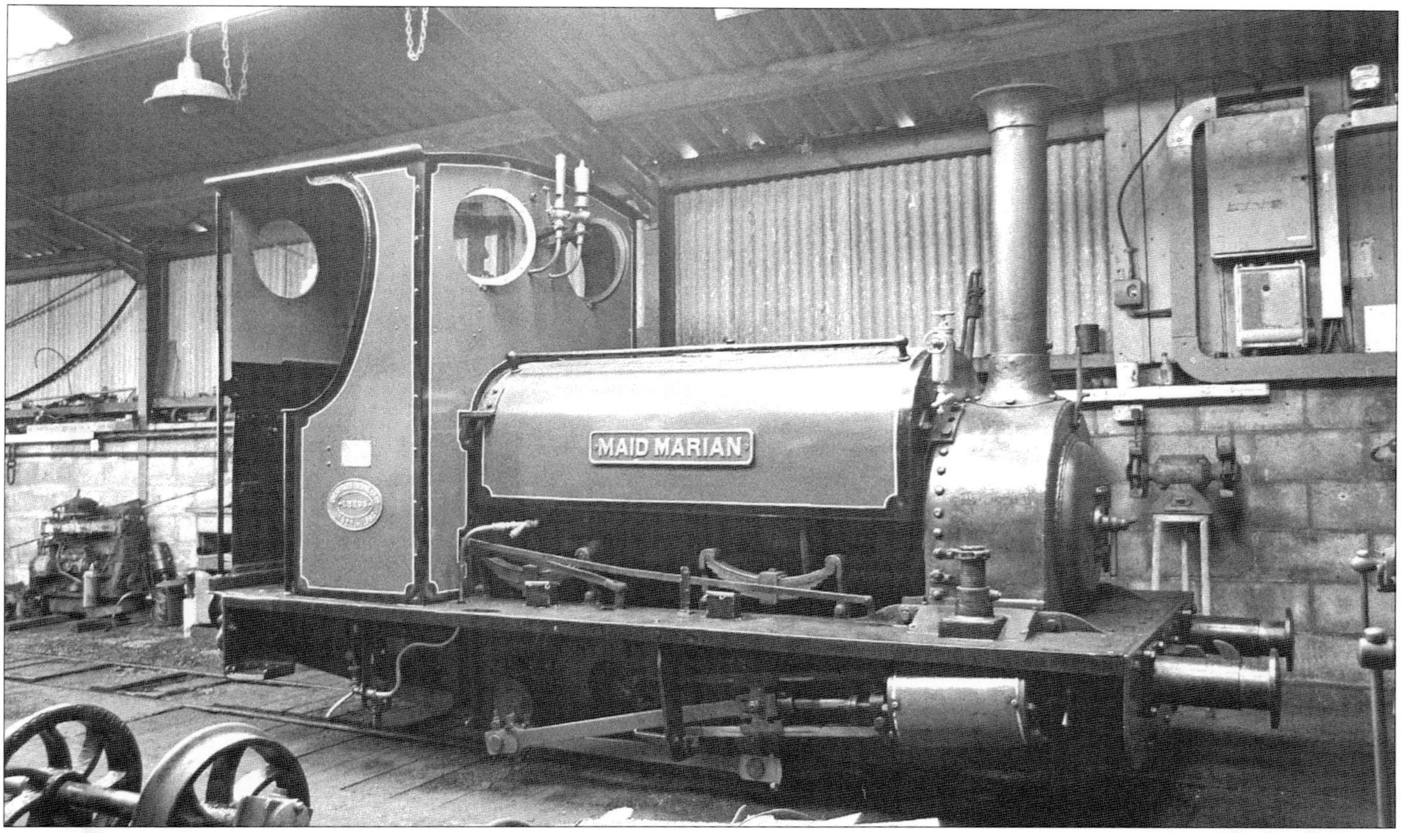
MAID MARIAN

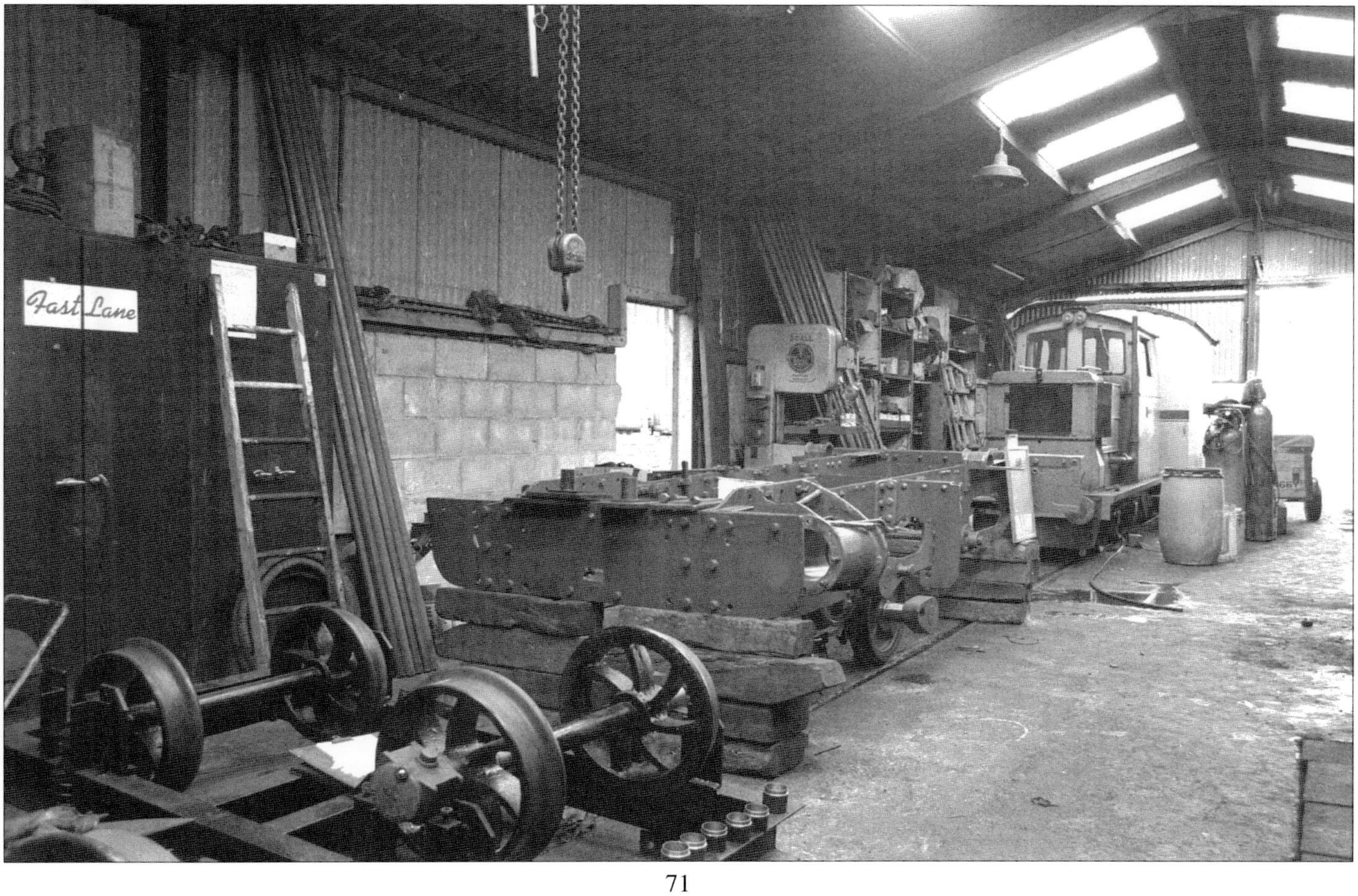
Fast Lane

A NARROW GAUGE VIEW OF NORTH WALES (1955-88)

"Holy War" and its train in open countryside (top) and entering Bryn Hynod (bottom) in summer 1988. All the coaches were built locally, the leading one (No 9) in 1982, the two centre coaches (Nos 6 and 7) in 1979 and the Brake coach (No 8) in 1981.

Talyllyn Railway

The Talyllyn Railway was the first of the slate carrying railways to be steam operated from inception. It was also to carry general merchandise and passengers. The line was built to a gauge of 2ft 3in along the Fathew Valley from Tywyn to Abergynolwyn. This was the extent of the line for passenger services, which commenced in 1866. Beyond here there was a freight and mineral line, the latter involving rope-operated inclines. At Tywyn, slate was transferred to the standard gauge Cambrian Railways, later the GWR. The quarries closed in 1947, but passenger services continued despite impending bankruptcy. The railway was rescued from closure by the formation of a preservation society in 1950. All the equipment was worn out, and in the early years the society brought this up to a reasonable standard. An extension for passenger services over part of the old mineral line was opened in 1976, giving a 7½-mile journey from Tywyn. The journey time is about three-quarters of an hour each way, with a service most of the year. In summer there are three trains in the morning and five in the afternoon.

Tywyn Wharf was originally used only for slate traffic, but later also became a passenger station. The railway's own two engines were both exhausted by the time the preservation society was formed. Two engines from the defunct Corris Railway were obtained in 1951. They retained their Corris numbers and one (No 4) is seen at Tywyn Wharf on 6th July 1959. This was named "Edward Thomas" by the Talyllyn Railway, after its one-time traffic manager. It was built in 1921, the ungainly chimney being fitted in 1958 as part of several modifications to improve performance; the original chimney was refitted in 1969. This collection of ancient 4-wheeled vehicles consists of a brake van (No 6), two former Glyn Valley Tramway coaches (now Nos 14 and 15), followed by Talyllyn Railway coaches (Nos 3 and 2) of 1866/67. The brake van is ex-Corris Railway No 11 (GWR No 8754), acquired by the Talyllyn Railway in 1951. A replacement body was fitted in 1958. There are opening doors only on the north side of coaches on the Talyllyn Railway due to limited clearances, a feature shared with the Corris Railway. The nearer open-sided bogie coach (No 13) is new, but the other open coach (No 7) was built about 1900 and obtained from the Penrhyn Railway in 1953. On the rear of the train are bogie coaches Nos 9 and 10 (see page 86).
Inset: Ticket from Towyn to Dolgoch, typical of the style issued prior to the Second World War.

A NARROW GAUGE VIEW OF NORTH WALES (1955-88)

Above: One of the original Talyllyn Railway engines, appropriately named "Talyllyn", at Tywyn Wharf in 1965. To the right is the standard gauge former Cambrian Railways line (later GWR and BR), alongside which is the narrow gauge slate transfer siding.

Left: "Edward Thomas" enters Wharf station on a train from Abergynolwyn on 5th July 1960. The vehicle behind the engine is the original Talyllyn Railway guard's van (No 5) built for the opening of the line. The open (toast rack) coaches near the front were built between 1957 and 1959. The first vehicle is one of a pair numbered 11 and 12 and the other is No 13. The two bogie coaches are Nos 10 and 9.

TALYLLYN RAILWAY

Above: "Edward Thomas" passing under the road bridge by Wharf station on a train up the valley in 1965. The recently built leading coach is No 18.

Right: At Pendre, on the outskirts of Tywyn, the railway has a small station, and servicing, storage and repair facilities. The engine shed is the stone building in the centre and the wooden building to the right is the carriage shed. The first wagon is side tipper No 50. The other two iron-bodied wagons (Nos 1 and 2) were both from the Corris Railway where they were numbers 13 and 12 (GWR Nos 31999 and 31998).

A NARROW GAUGE VIEW OF NORTH WALES (1955-88)

Left: The other former Corris Railway engine (No 3), built in 1878, was seen in Pendre Yard on 17th August 1955. After acquisition by the Talyllyn Railway it was named "Sir Haydn" after the local MP Sir Henry Haydn Jones, who was also owner of the quarry and the railway. As operator of Aberllefenni Quarry (see page 90) in the 1930s, Sir Haydn had also played an important part in the survival of the Corris Railway. It was withdrawn from service in 1958 and stored.

Below: "Sir Haydn" in the North Carriage Shed, awaiting rebuilding in 1960. It re-entered service in 1968. The wagon (No 21) in the foreground was originally a slate wagon, converted to a flat wagon at Pendre in 1951. It was scrapped ten years later.

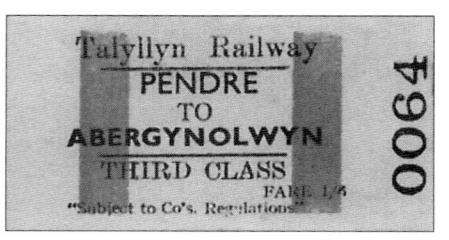

Above: Pendre to Abergynolwyn ticket, a typical 1950s issue. The base ticket (white or coloured) was often overprinted with one or more coloured stripes, in this instance a pale green ticket with brown stripes.

Left: One of the original Talyllyn Railway locomotives, No 1, built in 1864, had been in store for almost ten years when this photograph was taken in 1955. By this time, the shed was as decrepit as the locomotive, which was later rebuilt, and was in use again from 1958 to 1968. It was again rebuilt and re-entered service in 1972.

Below: This is "Talyllyn" (No 1) again, this time in the running shed in 1988. The engine behind is "Dolgoch" (No 2), which was built in 1866. It ceased to be used in the 1950s and was rebuilt in 1963. "Dolgoch" had been renamed "Pretoria" during the Boer War, but carried the name only briefly.

A NARROW GAUGE VIEW OF NORTH WALES (1955-88)

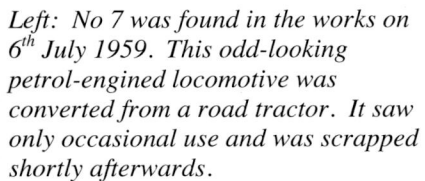

Left: No 7 was found in the works on 6th July 1959. This odd-looking petrol-engined locomotive was converted from a road tractor. It saw only occasional use and was scrapped shortly afterwards.

Below left: No 5 is a more conventional diesel locomotive, and was acquired by the Midland Area Group of the preservation society in 1956 from a quarry near Nuneaton, hence the name "Midlander". It is often used on engineers' trains, and is capable of working passenger trains. Diesel locomotives are, however, not normally used on the latter.

Opposite page top: Locomotive No 6, "Douglas", was built in 1918, and spent most of its life at RAF Calshot near Southampton, until the end of the Second World War. It arrived on the Talyllyn Railway in 1954, and is seen here in Pendre Yard in July 1960.

Opposite page bottom: A general view of the exterior of the works shows two more of the railway's small fleet of diesel locomotives. On the left is "Alf" (No 9), built in 1950, and owned by the National Coal Board for use in its mines. It came to the Talyllyn Railway in 1970. On the right is "Merseysider" (No 8), built in 1964, arriving on the Talyllyn Railway from a steel works in Rotherham five years later. The building in the centre is the South Carriage Shed.

Below: Ticket from Rhydyronen to Dolgoch. The base ticket is white, the top stripe a pale green and the bottom a mid green.

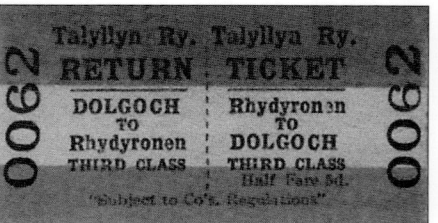

78

TALYLLYN RAILWAY

Top: A short distance beyond Pendre, the line begins the climb, passing through three halts to arrive at Rhydyronen, a little over two miles from Tywyn Wharf. The steepest section is at 1 in 71. "Dolgoch" approaches Rhydyronen in 1988. There was a siding on the right (see lower picture), where the platform is now located.

Bottom: Twenty-three years earlier, "Talyllyn" enters Rhydyronen on the down "Centenarian". The train was named to commemorate the Act of Parliament of 1865 sanctioning the construction of the line. The leading coach is No 10.

TALYLLYN RAILWAY

Top: Just beyond Rhydyronen, the line drops a short distance before levelling off and then resuming the climb to Brynglas. A siding was converted into a loop in 1953. "Talyllyn" approaches the station with an up train in 1988. The leading coach is No 20, built in 1970.

Bottom: "Dolgoch" crosses the minor road at the west end of Brynglas station on a train bound for Tywyn Wharf. Right: Ticket from Brynglas to Abergynolwyn.

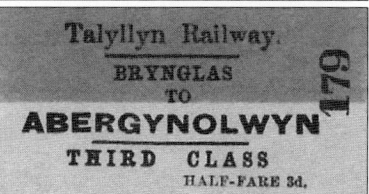

81

A NARROW GAUGE VIEW OF NORTH WALES (1955-88)

Above: It is almost two miles to the next station of Dolgoch, approached on a viaduct over a river of the same name. "Edward Thomas" takes water at Dolgoch before continuing its journey to Abergynolwyn in August 1955. The water tower ceased to be used regularly in 1961 when a new tower was built a few yards away.

Left: "Edward Thomas" in Dolgoch station four years later.

Oppostite page top: A little under half a mile beyond Dolgoch is Quarry Siding. There is also a passing loop (installed in 1968) and a halt here. "Talyllyn" crosses the unprotected road with a down train in the 1980s.

Opposite page bottom: "Sir Haydn" passes the loop at Quarry Siding in 1988.

Inset: Ticket from Dolgoch to Wharf.

TALYLLYN RAILWAY

83

Left: The siding is overgrown and contains a few stored wagons in 1988. The quarry had traditionally provided ballast for the Railway, but closed several years ago.

Below: "Dolgoch" deep in the woods near Quarry Siding.

Opposite page top: "Talyllyn" trundles down the valley between Abergynolwyn and Quarry Siding in 1988. The first coach is No 16, a bogie vehicle from Derbyshire, rebuilt several times at Pendre before taking on its present form. The second coach is one of the vehicles from the Glyn Valley Tramway, which closed in 1935. Both have been extensively rebuilt and now provide First Class accommodation (see page 73).

TALYLLYN RAILWAY

Later the same day, "Dolgoch" leads its train through open countryside near Abergynolwyn. The leading coach is No 17, built for the Corris Railway in 1898 and withdrawn in 1930. On disposal of Corris Railway assets, it was sold and used as a garden shed. It was rebuilt, using many new parts, and began service on the Talyllyn Railway in 1961.

A NARROW GAUGE VIEW OF NORTH WALES (1955-88)

Left: "Edward Thomas" with a train of bogie and four-wheeled stock at the terminus of Abergynolwyn on 6th July 1959 (see also page 73).

Bottom left: Abergynolwyn station was rebuilt in 1969 with improved passenger facilities. Further changes were made in 1976 when it became a through station. These included the provision of a siding and passing loop, and lengthening of the platform. This enables an up and a down train to use the platform simultaneously. "Talyllyn" enters Abergynolwyn in summer 1988.

Below: Ticket from Abergynolwyn to Rhydyronen

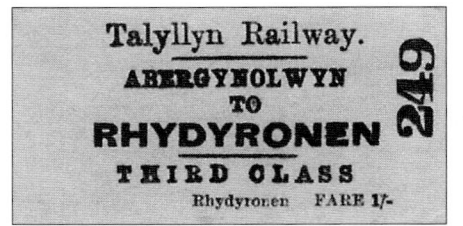

Top: The same train preparing to leave for Nant Gwernol.
Bottom: "Dolgoch" stands at Abergynolwyn awaiting departure to Tywyn in 1988.

A NARROW GAUGE VIEW OF NORTH WALES (1955-88)

Above: The current end of the line at Nant Gwernol looking toward the Allt-wyllt Incline. Although the track has been removed from the incline, there is a footpath to the top. Several other footpaths also start from Nant Gwernol station.

Opposite page top: The extension to Nant Gwernol was begun in 1970, and it was six years before the new line was opened. Much of the area is wooded, and there is a network of footpaths that are open to the public. There are also various unmade roads, but these are restricted to Forestry Commission vehicles. One such road crosses the railway at a place, uninspiringly, called Forestry Crossing. "Sir Haydn" is seen here twelve years after opening of the extension.

Opposite page bottom: "Dolgoch" descends from Nant Gwernol toward Abergynolwyn on the same day. There is a footpath between Abergynolwyn and Nant Gwernol, which uses Forestry Crossing.

Right: Single ticket from Nant Gwernol to Abergynolwyn, issued on 18th July 1988.

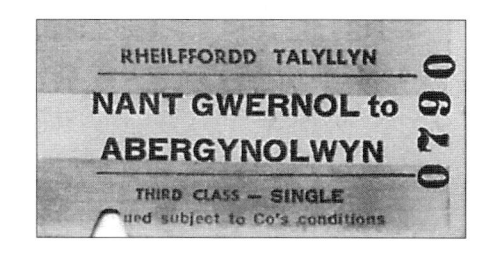

Corris Railway

A tramway to a gauge of 2ft 3in was opened in 1859 in order to transport slate from the quarries in the Aberllefenni area, down the Dulas Valley to a quay on the Afon Dyfi (River Dovey) for onward transhipment. Steam engines did not arrive on the line until 1878. Passenger services were introduced officially in 1883 between Machynlleth and Corris, and extended further up the valley to Aberllefenni in 1887. There had been semi-official horse-operated passenger services in the 1870s, which were suspended from 1878 while matters were regularised. There were tramways further up the Dulas Valley and in the Deri Valley, and these remained horse-worked mineral lines. The passenger service from Machynlleth and Aberllefenni lasted until the beginning of 1931. The railway had been purchased by the GWR the previous year, and passed into BR ownership on 1st January 1948. The railway lasted only a few more months, and was closed completely in August 1948, followed by demolition and disposal of assets (see page 73). A few buildings survived, including the station at Machynlleth and the engine shed at Maespoeth, which became used for other purposes. It was assumed that trains would never run again. However, following decades of work by the Corris Railway Society, trains returned to the line (albeit only between Maespoeth and Corris), in April 1985. Passenger services recommenced in the summer of 2002. A new steam engine, similar to the original Corris Railway No 4, was delivered in 2005. An extension south to a new terminus near the Centre for Alternative Technology is planned.

Machynlleth station survived the demolition of the railway and a visit in 1988 found it being used by a cycle hire company. An appropriate use, particularly as there could be little difference in journey time along the Dulas Valley whether by train or cycle. In the background of both pictures is the old goods shed, beyond which used to be the carriage shed. The Cambrian Railways (later GWR and BR) station is a few minutes walk away.

Opposite page top: The first station was at Ffridd Gate (closed by 1925), located shortly after the railway crossed the Afon Dyfi. The second station was at Llywyngwern, seen here in 1988. Little remains other than the station waiting room. The adjacent bus stop and the car act as reminders of some of the reasons for the demise of the railway. The road has been realigned and encroaches on to the trackbed at some locations. Here the trackbed hosts the signpost. There was a siding to Llywyngwern Quarry, which is now occupied by the Centre for Alternative Technology.

CORRIS RAILWAY

Left: Three and a half miles from Machynlleth was Esgairgeiliog station, the remains of which are seen in 1988 looking up the valley toward Corris. The station has since been restored and is awaiting the return of the train.

Right: Tickets from Machynlleth to Ffridd Gate and from Esgairgeiliog to Garneddwen, both typical of those in use in the early 1900s.
(Corris Railway Society Collection)

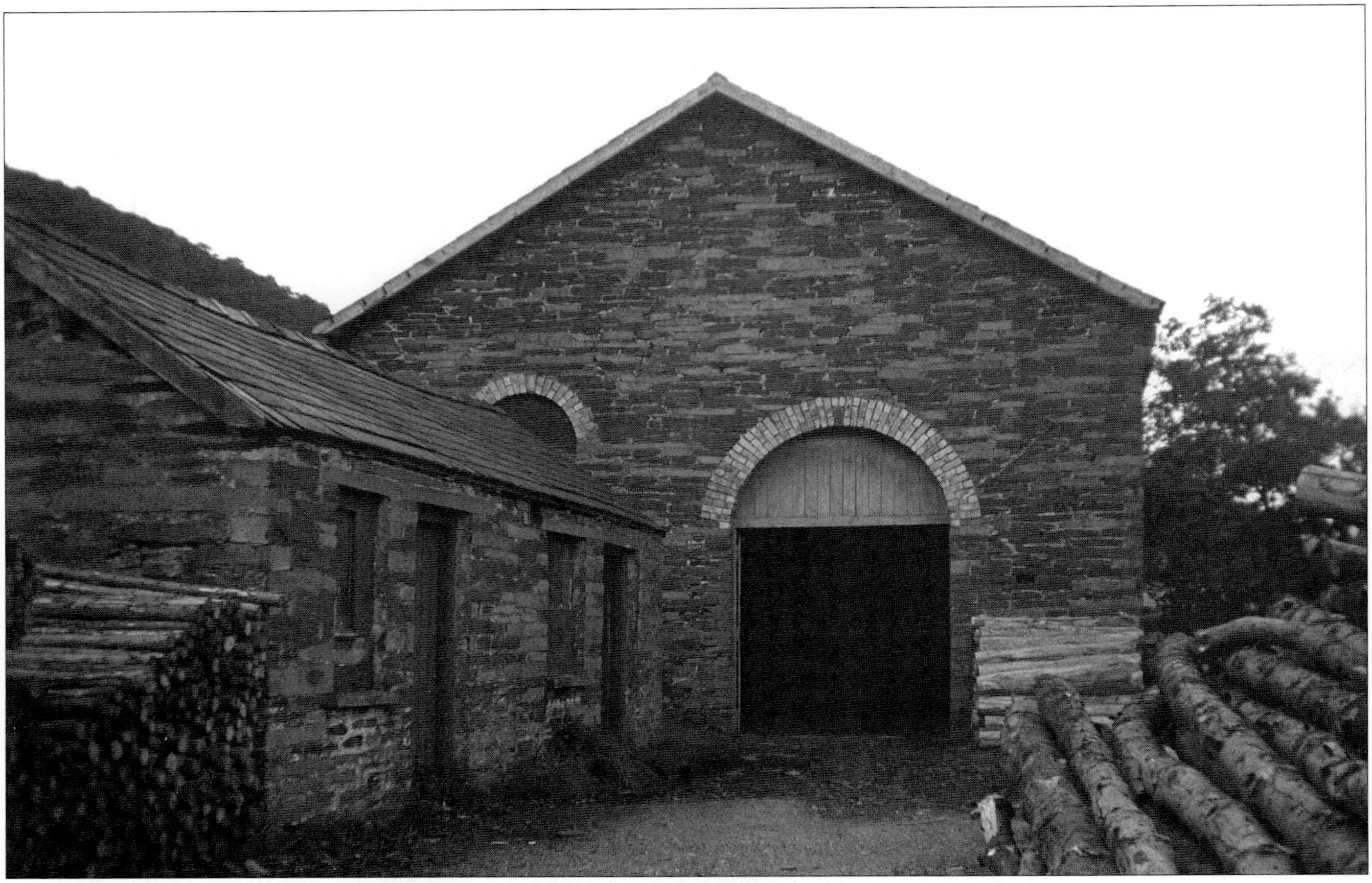

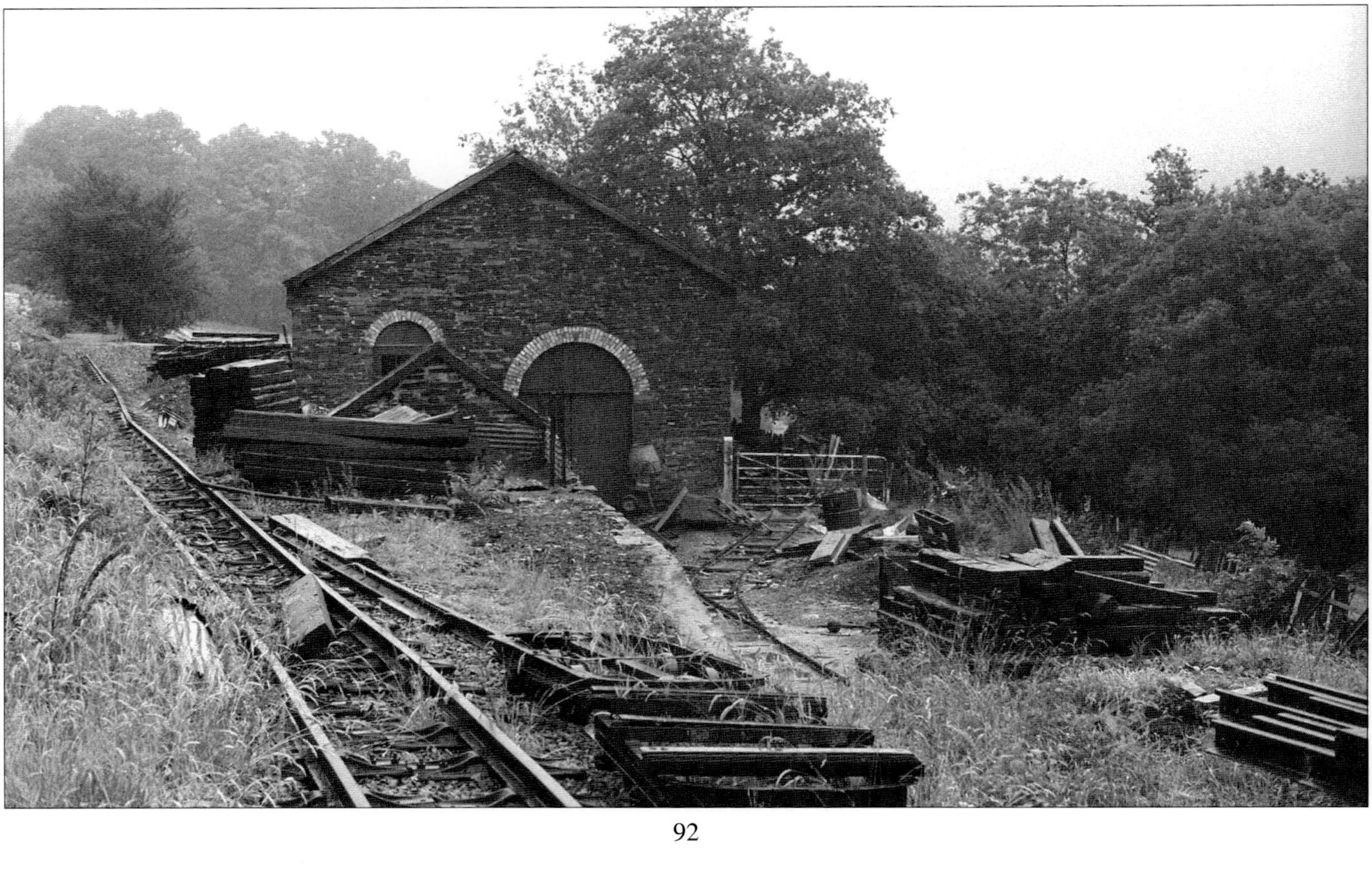

Opposite page top: Although there was never a station at Maespoeth, it was the junction for the horse-worked Upper Corris branch, which served several quarries in the Valley. There was no passenger service on the branch. There was also an engine shed at Maespoeth, which was used by the Forestry Commission for many years following closure of the line, as seen here in August 1955.

Opposite page bottom: The engine shed was acquired by the Corris Railway Society in 1981. Changes are taking place over seven years later and there is clear evidence of the rebirth of the railway. To the left was the tramway to Upper Corris and to the right the "main" line to Corris and Aberllefenni.

Above right: Alongside the shed on the same day.

Middle: Looking south from the site of Corris station in 1988 shows that the track has been laid past the church on the right, toward Maespoeth. This location has subsequently become the terminus of reinstated passenger services, and as a result has a much tidier appearance.

Below right: Corris station was demolished in 1968, but the adjacent stables have become the Corris Railway Museum, which was opened in 1970. The stables, which closed in 1949, were for the horses used on the tramways and for the railway's road vehicles.

Top: Beyond Aberllefenni, the line became a tramway. Looking south, the tramway trackbed passes a chapel and, just round the corner, the site of Aberllefenni station.
Bottom: Looking north beyond Aberllefenni station, the course of the Aberllefenni Quarry tramway crosses the road in front of the houses. The Ratgoed tramway ran round the rear of the houses. A slate works was situated to the right rear.

CORRIS RAILWAY

Right: This quarry hut at Aberllefenni with the bell was the wages office. The tramway went behind the hut, not through the gate to the left, then swung right over the road to Ratgoed Quarries.

Below: The tramway from Maespoeth Junction along the Deri Valley crossed the A487 on the bridge on the left. The tramway to Upper Corris passed under the bridge alongside the road. The bridge itself carried a tramway branch into Braichgoch Quarry. The incline was used to transfer slate from the quarries to the cutting sheds below. Rising from right to left across the photograph is a minor road linking Corris with Upper Corris. Major changes have taken place since this 1955 view. Following closure of the quarries, the area was landscaped and the main road re-routed.

Welshpool & Llanfair Light Railway

The line was built almost parallel to the road from Welshpool, running west to Llanfair Caereinion. For much of the way, it also runs close to the Sylfaen Brook and the Afon Banwy. It was opened in April 1903, and operated by Cambrian Railways. The line was 9 miles long, with six intermediate stations and halts, and to a gauge of 2ft 6in. It was built for the carriage of general merchandise, farm supplies, timber and passengers. Two further halts were subsequently built. The line became part of the GWR in 1923, which withdrew passenger services in 1931. Goods continued until complete closure of the line by BR in 1956. A preservation company reinstated passenger services between Llanfair Caereinion and Castle Caereinion in 1963. Further sections were opened in 1972 and 1981, but it was not feasible to reopen the last remaining section of the line, which used to run through the streets of Welshpool. Journey time is about fifty minutes each way, with one morning and two or three afternoon trains from April to October.

This page top: The narrow and standard gauge stations at Welshpool were adjacent. There was also an engine shed, goods yard and transfer sidings. A visit in August 1955 found all the cattle wagons that the railway possessed. Two were built in 1902 (GWR Nos 13623 and 13626) and the other two (Nos 38088 and 38089) in 1923. The cattle dock is in the background. The goods brake van on the left is one of two built in 1902, numbered 1 and 2 (later GWR Nos 8759 and 8755 respectively).

This page bottom: No track remained in 1988, although the cattle dock is still extant.

Opposite page top: There was, however, a remnant of track nearby. In the background is the BR standard gauge line.

Opposite page bottom: The railway possessed only two engines and these were both dead on shed on 13th August 1955. No 823 is in the front and No 822 hidden behind. Both survived closure and are currently in use on the revitalised railway.

WELSHPOOL & LLANFAIR LIGHT RAILWAY

A NARROW GAUGE VIEW OF NORTH WALES (1955-88)

Left: In 1981, a new terminus was built on the outskirts of Welshpool at Raven Square, just west of the original intermediate station of the same name. "The Countess" (ex-BR No 823) departs from Raven Square in the summer of 1988.

Below: "The Countess" tackles the first of several climbs on it way to Llanfair. This is Golfa Bank which starts just after Raven Square, and is at 1 in 39, steepening to 1 in 29, then easing before the site of Golfa station. No original passenger stock has survived, so coaches had to be obtained from other sources. The first coach of this train is No B17 built in 1901, and one of four 4-wheelers donated to the railway by the Zillertalbahn of Austria in 1968. A further coach (No B27) followed in 1975. The next coach, a bogie First Class No 1207, was built in England in 1961 and shipped to Sierra Leone. It was acquired by the WLLR in 1975, and for a time was named "Ursula". The last coach (B24, see opposite) is also from Austria and was modified after acquisition to include a guard's compartment.

Top: The highest point on the line lies between Golfa and Sylfaen. A train bound for Llanfair enters the latter station in summer 1988. Trains started to run from Llanfair as far as here in 1972; a loop was added in 1976. It was not until nine years later that services were extended to Raven Square.
Bottom: "The Countess" approaches Castle Caereinion, almost four miles from Raven Square.

Several passengers board at Castle Caereinion. There is a signal box and waiting shelter, the former being installed in 1907. The waiting shelter replaced an earlier corrugated iron building.

Left: Some trains were running only from Llanfair to Cyfronydd on a special occasion in 1988. This was to mark the Silver Jubilee of the reopening of the railway. The two open bogie wagons loaded with sleepers were obtained from the Admiralty in 1961 and modified to suit their new role.

Below: The same train prepares to return to Llanfair. The waiting shelter on the right is the body of an ex-LNWR brake van.

A NARROW GAUGE VIEW OF NORTH WALES (1955-88)

Left: Leaving Cyfronydd for Llanfair.

Below: About a mile west of Cyfronydd, the railway crosses the Afon Banwy, and a train is seen here during Jubilee year.

Opposite page top: A short distance beyond the bridge is Heniarth. "The Countess" indulges in some shunting in the station yard in 1965. The previous winter had seen severe flood damage to the bridge over the Afon Banwy and no trains could run further east than Heniarth until late summer 1965. The open wagon No 7 (BR No 71794) has since been used for spare parts to repair similar wagons. The goods brake van is No 2 (BR No 8755), see page 96.

Opposite page bottom: Earlier in the year "The Earl" (No 1) was working the passenger service between Llanfair and Heniarth. The river bridge can be seen in the background.

WELSHPOOL & LLANFAIR LIGHT RAILWAY

A NARROW GAUGE VIEW OF NORTH WALES (1955-88)

Above: There are eight level crossings, all over minor roads, between Raven Square and Llanfair. "The Countess" seems to emerge from behind a hedge at one such crossing.

Left: Trains are hemmed in on both sides on the section of line between Heniarth and Llanfair. This is "The Countess" heading for Llanfair in 1965.

Opposite page top: From 1931, water was taken from a tower alongside the Afon Banwy just east of Llanfair. The tower was gravity-fed from a sump in a stream above the railway, although water was occasionally pumped from the river in times of drought. "The Countess" takes water from here in 1965. This practice ceased in 1979 when a new water tower was built at Llanfair itself.

Opposite page bottom: Arrival of "The Countess" at Llanfair in 1988. The steam engine to the right of the train is "Dougal" (No 8). It was built in Scotland in 1946, and arrived on the WLLR in 1969. The diesel locomotive on the far right is "Chattenden" (No 7).

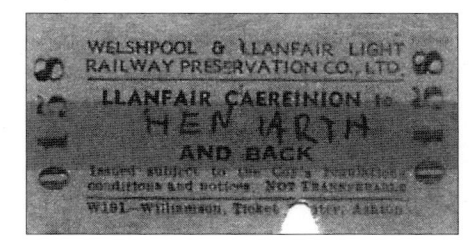

Return ticket Llanfair Caereinion to Heniarth, issued 3rd June 1965.

A NARROW GAUGE VIEW OF NORTH WALES (1955-88)

WELSHPOOL & LLANFAIR LIGHT RAILWAY

Opposite page top: "The Earl" leaves for Heniarth in 1965 with a three coach train consisting of a bogie brake composite coach No 214, a bogie 5-compartment coach No 204 and a 4-wheeled guard's van No 213; all were from the Admiralty. No 214 has separate compartments for officers and NCOs. It was rebuilt by the WLLR as a closed coach from the original open "toast rack" style. This coach, and three others of the same style, were sold in 1978 to the Sittingbourne & Kemsley Light Railway. No 214 went to the South Tynedale Railway in 1989, and was subsequently bought by the Welsh Highland Railway.

Opposite page bottom: A view from the end of the line. The locomotive is "Orion" (No 15) built in Belgium in 1948 and used in Finland until the 1970s. It arrived on the WLLR in 1983. The coaches on the left and right are both of Austrian origin.

Top right: "The Countess". The two original engines were named after the Earl and Countess of Powis. The Earl had provided land for the railway and was one of its directors.

Middle right: A contrast in ancient and modern. The cattle wagon is No 38088 from 1902 and the locomotive is "Chattenden", built in 1949 for the Admiralty, and purchased by the WLLR in 1968.

Bottom right: A general view of the station and workshops looking west. The workshops and shed opened in 1970. The new water tower is just to the right of the workshops.

A NARROW GAUGE VIEW OF NORTH WALES (1955-88)

WELSHPOOL & LLANFAIR LIGHT RAILWAY

Opposite page top: "Dougal", dwarfed by Austrian coach No B16 and one of the coaches from Sierra Leone (No 1066).

Opposite page bottom: The two out-of-use engines are No 14 and "Monarch" (No 6). No 14 was built in Leeds in 1954, and was one of the Sierra Leone Government Railway fleet. It was purchased by the WLLR in 1975. "Monarch", an articulated locomotive, was built in 1953 and worked in Kent until 1965 and arrived at Llanfair a year later.

This page, both photographs: "The Countess" being coaled by hand in Llanfair yard.

Vale of Rheidol Railway

The railway was built for the transport of both goods and passengers. There were several lead mines in the Vale of Rheidol, and the ore was transported by rail to Aberystwyth and beyond. Sidings to transfer ore to the Cambrian Railways were provided at Aberystwyth. There was also a short branch to Rotfawr Wharf on Aberystwyth Harbour for the transhipment of ore. Mineral traffic virtually ceased by the mid-1920s and the Harbour branch closed.

Passengers were expected to be local people and tourists on day trips from the developing resort of Aberystwyth, to Devil's Bridge and the various waterfalls in the vicinity. The line was built to a gauge of 1ft 11½in, and was opened for goods traffic in the summer of 1902, followed by passenger trains at the end of the same year. There were four intermediate stations, with three halts added within two years. Another intermediate halt was added in 1910. The Vale of Rheidol Railway was taken over by the Cambrian Railways in 1913, and this in turn was absorbed into the GWR ten years later. In 1948, the line became part of the BR network. Even this was not the final change, as it was sold by BR in 1989.

Journey time is one hour each way for a distance of twelve miles. There is no service in the winter months. Peak service sees four trains per day and two per day in spring and autumn.

The train crew chat with a colleague as "Llywelyn" (No 8) waits for departure time to Devil's Bridge in July 1959. The leading coach, No 4994 (VR No 10) was built in 1938, along with six other similar Third Class vehicles. The railway has probably had more relocations of termini than any other. This is the second station, and was situated alongside the standard gauge station, also a terminus. The original station, situated a short distance to the west, was closed in 1925.

Above: The station was moved again in 1968, to be within the BR station, by using the Carmarthen line platform. The line to Carmarthen had closed two years previously. Here "Owain Glyndŵr" (No 7) waits at the buffer stops, before retiring to the engine shed. In the background is BR unit No 150 122, forming a train to Shrewsbury. There were plans to move the station yet again, to a location near the former GWR standard gauge engine shed, but these have not yet come to fruition.

Left: 'Vale of Rheidol' notice.

Below: Aberystwyth to Devil's Bridge ticket issued in the 1980s.

A NARROW GAUGE VIEW OF NORTH WALES (1955-88)

Above: Occasional extra trains were run and this is the "Night Rheidol". "Owain Glyndŵr" backs on to the stock, watched by a crowd of intending passengers in the last year of BR ownership. In 1983, the engine had been repainted in BR lined green with the lion and wheel emblem. The open sided coach to the right is No 4151 (VR No 9), built in 1938 in anticipation of fine weather throughout subsequent summers.

Left: In July 1959, No 9 is in the engine shed at Aberystwyth. This was former GWR No 1213, and was built in 1902. It carried the name "Prince of Wales" until 1915, and again from 1956. Sister engine No 1212 only survived until 1938, when it was scrapped. All three surviving locomotives were repainted in BR Rail Blue livery in 1967, and were the only steam engines in BR ownership ever to carry this livery.

VALE OF RHEIDOL RAILWAY

Above: Not content with relocating its station, the Railway also moved engine sheds. The old shed was closed in 1968, and operations transferred to the former standard gauge engine shed, built by the GWR in 1938. This is used for stabling and repairs of rolling stock and motive power. "Prince of Wales" (No 9) is seen in its new home in 1988. It had been repainted in ochre, the original Vale of Rheidol Railway colours, in 1982.

Right: "Owain Glyndŵr" is undergoing repairs inside the new premises. There is a glimpse of the future, with a diesel locomotive (No 10) hiding behind the steam engine.

113

A NARROW GAUGE VIEW OF NORTH WALES (1955-88)

Left: No 10 had only been in BR ownership a matter of weeks before this photograph was taken inside the shed in 1988. Behind the engine is a 4-wheeled guard's van, No 137 (VR No 19), which was built in 1938 using the underframe of an earlier vehicle.

Below: An unnamed No 8 is in smart but simple Cambrian Railways livery, shunting a few coaches into the shed in 1988. The locomotive had been named "Llywelyn" in 1956, but the nameplates were removed when it lost its BR livery in 1986. After Nationalisation, the locomotive was painted in lined green with the BR lion and wheel emblem, Rail Blue in 1967, GWR livery in 1981 and the present (1988) livery in 1986.

Top: Taking water on a wet day. A reflection of No 8 outside the shed.
Bottom: Preparation for the next journey up the valley.

A NARROW GAUGE VIEW OF NORTH WALES (1955-88)

VALE OF RHEIDOL RAILWAY

Opposite page top: "Owain Glyndŵr" is in early BR livery, but the year is 1988. Nos 7 and 8 were built by the GWR in 1923 to the same basic design as the earlier locomotive (now No 9), but with some improvements.

Opposite page bottom: General view of the shed and yard. The two 4-wheeled bolster wagons in the foreground are Nos W8510 and W34106, rebuilt by the GWR from end-door open wagons obtained from the Hafan & Talybont Tramway in 1901. The third wagon in the row is from the same source and is end-opening for loco coal. The first of the coaches is No 4150 (VR No 8), built by the GWR in 1938. All coaches were allocated a local number (one or two digit) and a stock number (four digits) by the GWR. At Nationalisation, the prefix and suffix "W" were added to the latter number. On transfer of the line to the Midland Region, the prefix was changed to "M". Several coaches were repainted in GWR chocolate and cream in 1983, when the letters were omitted.

Above: "Owain Glyndŵr" passes Aberystwyth shed on an afternoon train from Devil's Bridge. The leading coach is 4996 (VR No 12), built in 1938 as a Brake Third. Some compartments were converted to First Class in 1983 when First Class travel first became available on the Railway.

Above and left: Just beyond Llanbadarn Halt the railway crosses the Afon Rheidol. "Owain Glyndŵr" is seen here on a train from Devil's Bridge in the late 1980s.

Opposite page top: Lovesgrove station, which closed in 1914, was situated 3¼ miles from Aberystwyth. Near here is No 8 on an up train in 1988. The leading coach is No 4148 (VR No 6), a Second Class vehicle built at Swindon in 1938.

Opposite page bottom: No 8 is seen on another up train earlier in the day, just beyond Capel Bangor. The bridge in the background takes a minor road over the Afon Rheidol, but the railway and road cross on the level. Shortly beyond Capel Bangor, the train meets the first of several climbs at 1 in 50, which after a pause steepens to 1 in 48 before reaching the next station of Nantyronen.

VALE OF RHEIDOL RAILWAY

Top: "Owain Glyndŵr" approaches Nantyronen on an up train in the summer of 1988.

Bottom: When the line first opened, engines took water at Nantyronen on the up journey. This was soon abandoned in favour of the next station of Aberffrwd. Watering facilities were re-established at Nantyronen in 1982. "Owain Glyndŵr" takes water here in 1988.

Opposite page: "Prince of Wales" takes water at Aberffrwd in the summer of 1960. The line is level through Aberffrwd. The loop was closed in 1963, so trains could no longer pass anywhere along the line. It was reinstated in 1990.

VALE OF RHEIDOL RAILWAY

A NARROW GAUGE VIEW OF NORTH WALES (1955-88)

Left: Having replenished its tanks, "Owain Glyndŵr" is ready to tackle the next 1 in 50 climb.

Middle: In spring 1965 "Owain Glyndŵr" attacks the gradient beyond Aberffrwd, and produces a huge pall of smoke as a result.

Bottom: No 8 thunders up the 1 in 50 gradient near Rhiwfron, which incorporates a sharp curve complete with check rail.

Below: BR return ticket from Aberystwyth to Devil's Bridge.

122

VALE OF RHEIDOL RAILWAY

Right: There is an excellent vantage point between Rhiwfron and Devil's Bridge from which to view both up and down trains. No 8 works an up train at this point in July 1988. The leading coach is No 4148.

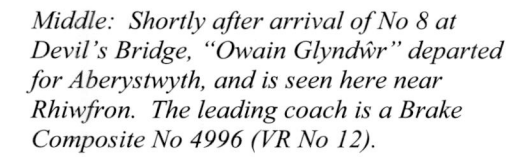

Middle: Shortly after arrival of No 8 at Devil's Bridge, "Owain Glyndŵr" departed for Aberystwyth, and is seen here near Rhiwfron. The leading coach is a Brake Composite No 4996 (VR No 12).

Bottom: No 7 arrives at Devil's Bridge on 19th August 1955. This engine was not named "Owain Glyndŵr" until the following year.

A NARROW GAUGE VIEW OF NORTH WALES (1955-88)

Opposite page top: This general view of Devil's Bridge station shows the simple layout and basic facilities. The layout changed in the 1960s when two sidings were removed. The remaining siding was extended behind the main station building in order to berth stock. The original building still stands and includes a gift shop. The ugly building to the left is a refreshment room, which was erected in 1978. The plaque on the station nameboard declares that it is 639ft above sea level, although elsewhere it is recorded as 680ft.

Opposite page bottom: Watering facilities are not within the station area, but the other side of an overbridge at the west end of the station. Here No 8 takes water in July 1988.

This page: No 8 in 1955 and again in 1959, now also known as "Llywelyn".

"Owain Glyndŵr" departs for Aberystwyth in summer 1965. Note the 'VR' on the coach sides, which were painted in Cambrian green. This had been applied the previous year, but was shortlived, and the coaches were repainted blue in 1968.

Index

Aberdovey (Aberdyfi), 56
Aberffrwd, 120-122
Aberglaslyn, 1, 36-38, 57
Abergynowlyn, 73, 74, 77, 81, 82, 84-89
Aberllefenni, 76, 90, 94
Aberystwyth, 1, 11, 110-118, 126
Afon Banwy, 96, 102, 104
Afon Dyfi, 90
Afon Glaslyn, 39
Afon Rheidol, 118
Afonwen, 64
Allt-wyllt Incline, 89

Bala Junction, 64, 68
Bala Lake, 1, 68
Bala Lake Railway, 12, 68-72
Bangor, 3
Barmouth, 1
Beddgelert, 35-37
Bethesda, 3, 5
Blaenau Ffestiniog, 1, 2, 9, 47, 56, 64, 67
Boston Lodge, 1, 47, 49, 50, 53, 55, 58, 59, 63
Braichgoch Quarry, 95
Brecon Mountain Railway, 2
Bredgar & Wormshill Railway, 11
British Railways, 2, 64, 73, 90, 96, 97, 110-112, 114, 116, 117, 127
Bryn Hynod, 68, 72
Brynglas, 81
Bryngwyn, 35

Caernarfon, 35
Cambrian Coast Line, 1, 2
Cambrian Railways, 73, 90, 96, 110
Campbell's Platform, 63
Capel Bangor, 118, 119
Carmarthen, 111
Castle Caereinion, 96, 99, 100
Cei Llyndan, 13, 21
Centre for Alternative Technology, 90
Clogwyn, 34
Coaches
    4-wheeled, 61, 73, 74

Coaches *(cont)*
    Bogie, 30, 31, 47, 48, 50, 67, 72, 81, 85, 98, 106, 112, 116-118, 123, 126
Cob, The, 49, 50, 52, 56
Coed-y-parc, 9
Conwy Valley, 10, 11
Corris, 1, 90-95
Corris Railway, 1, 73, 75, 85, 90-94
Corwen, 1
Creuau Bank, 61
Croesor, 35, 39
Cyfronydd, 101, 102

Ddault, 47, 60, 63
Deri Valley, 90, 93, 94
Devil's Bridge, 1, 110, 111, 117, 118, 125-125
Dinas Junction, 35, 43
Dinorwic Quarries, 1, 13-21, 27
Dinorwic Quarries Railway, 1, 70
Dolgellau, 68
Dolgoch, 82, 83
Duffws, 56, 64
Dulas Valley, 90

Esgairgeiliog, 91

Fairbourne Railway, 2
Fathew Valley, 73
Ffestiniog Railway, 1, 2, 9, 35, 40, 43, 47-67
Ffridd Gate, 90
Flag, 68
Forestry Commission, 88, 89, 92, 93

Garneddwen, 91
Garreg, 38, 39, 57
Gelert's Farm, 35, 40, 42-46
Gilfach Ddu, 13, 16-19, 21
Glanllyn, 68
Glyn Valley Tramway, 2, 73, 84
Golfa, 98, 99
Great Orme Tramway, 2
Great Western Railway, 35, 40, 41, 47, 56, 64, 68, 73, 90, 96, 110-114, 116, 117

Hafod-y-llyn, 38
Halfway, 22, 31-33
Hebron, 22, 30, 31
Heniarth, 102-104, 106, 107

Isle of Man Railway, 67

Launceston Steam Railway, 12
Llanbadarn Halt, 118
Llanberis, 1, 13, 22-29
Llanberis Lake Railway, 13-21
Llandudno, 64, 66
Llanfair Caereinion, 96, 98, 101-109
Llanfair P.G., 127
Llangower, 68
Llanuwchllyn, 68, 69
Llechwedd Slate Caverns, 66
Llyn Padarn, 1, 13
Llyn Quellyn, 35
Llywyngwern, 90
Locomotives
    Alf (No 9), 78, 79
    Alice, 70, 71
    Aylwin (No 7), 25
    Blanche, 9, 61
    Cegin, 7
    Charles, 9
    Chattenden (No 7), 104, 105, 107
    Chilmark, 70, 71
    Countess, The (Nos 2 and 823), 97-107, 109
    Dolbadarn, 20, 21
    Dolgoch (No 2), iii, 77, 80, 84, 85, 87
    Dougal (No 8), 104, 105, 108, 109
    Douglas (No 6), 78, 79
    Earl of Merioneth, 62, 63
    Earl, The (Nos 1 and 822), 97, 102, 103, 106, 107
    Edward Sholto, 12
    Edward Thomas (No 4), 73, 74, 82, 86
    Eigiau, 11
    Elidir, 14-17, 21
    Enid, 16
    Enid (No 2), 23, 24, 30, 31
    Eryri (No 7), 25

Vale of Rheidol platform ticket BR(M), issued on 6th June 1965. The line came under the Midland Region of BR from 1963, hence the suffix "M" on the platform ticket. As far as is known the only other platform ticket anywhere in the British Isles that at the time cost more than 1d was issued at Llanfair P.G.

A NARROW GAUGE VIEW OF NORTH WALES (1955-88)

Locomotives *(cont)*
  Gelert, 46
  George Henry, 11
  Glaslyn (No 1), 42, 44, 45
  Harold Wilson, 55
  Holy War, 69, 70, 72
  Iarll Meirionnydd, 62, 63
  Jubilee 1897, 11, 12
  Karen, 46
  Kathleen, 11
  Ladas (No 1), 25
  Lilian, 12
  Lilla, 12
  Linda, 9, 49, 50, 52, 57, 59-61, 63
  Llywelyn (No 8), 110, 114, 115, 118, 119, 122-125
  Maid Marian, 70, 71
  Marchlyn, 5, 6
  Meirionnydd, 69
  Merseysider (No 8), 78
  Midlander (No 5), 78
  Moel Siabod (No 5), 22, 27, 31
  Moelwyn, 55
  Moel Tryfan, 46
  Monarch (No 6), 108, 109
  Mountaineer, 58, 63, 67
  Ninian (No 9), 23
  Orion (No 15), 106, 107
  Owain Glyndŵr (No 7), 111-113, 116-118, 120, 122, 123, 126
  Padarn (No 6), 24, 31
  Palmerston, 53, 55
  Pretoria, 77
  Prince, 47, 48, 50, 57, 60, 66, 67
  Prince of Wales (Nos 9 and 1213), 112, 113, 120, 121
  Princess, 50
  Ralph Sadler (No 7), 25
  Red Damsel, 16
  Russell, 40, 41, 43-45
  Sandford, 9
  Sgt Murphy, 10
  Sir Haydn (No 3), 76, 82, 83, 88, 89
  Snowdon (No 4), 25
  Stanhope, 10
  Taliesin, 48-50, 53, 54, 56
  Talyllyn (No 1), 74, 77, 80-84, 86, 87
  Una, 16
  Upnor Castle, 50, 51
  Winifred, 8
  Wyddfa (No 3), 22, 28, 29
  Yeti (No 10), 29
  No 7, 78
  No 10, 113
  No 14, 108, 109

London & North Western Railway, 47, 64, 101
London, Midland & Scottish Railway, 35, 64, 65
Lovesgrove, 118, 119
Lynton & Barnstaple Railway, 57

Machynlleth, 1, 90, 91
Maentwrog, 56
Maespoeth, 1, 90, 92, 93, 95
Minffordd, 47, 56-58, 64
Museums
  Conwy Valley, 10
  Corris Railway, 93
  Narrow Gauge Railway, 11, 43
  Penrhyn Castle, 9, 13
  Welsh Slate, 13, 16

Nant Gwernol, 87-89
Nantlle, 16
Nantmor, 38, 39
Nantyronen, 118-120
North Wales Narrow Gauge Railways, 35-43

Oakeley Quarries, 19, 64, 65

Padarn Country Park, 19
Padarn Railway, 13-21
Pen Cob Halt, 50
Penllyn, 13, 21
Penrhyn Railway, 3-12, 50, 52, 73
Penrhyndeudreath (Penrhyn), 38, 57, 58
Pentrepiod, 68
Pen-y-bont, 68, 69
Penymount, 40
Pen-yr-orsedd, 16
Plas, 58
Port Dinorwic, 13, 19, 21
Port Penrhyn, 1, 3, 9
Porthmadog (Portmadoc), 1, 35, 39-41, 46-52, 56, 60-64, 66, 67
Princess May Level, 8
Purbeck, Isle of, 43

Quarry Siding, 82-84
Quellyn, 35

Ratgoed Quarries, 94, 95
Raven Square, 98, 99, 104
Red Lion Level, 3
Rhiwfron, 122, 123
Rhyd Ddu, 35
Rhydyronen, 80, 81, 86
Rocky Valley, 22
Rotfawr Wharf, 110

Shrewsbury, 1, 111
Sittingbourne & Kemsley Light Railway, 106, 107
Snowdon, 1, 22, 23, 27, 29-31, 34, 35
Snowdon Mountain Railway, 1, 13, 22-34
Snowdon Ranger, 1, 35
Snowdonia National Park, 60
Sylfaen, 96, 99

Talyllyn Railway, 2, 73-89
Tan-y-bwlch, 1, 47, 48, 50, 51, 56-63
Tanygrisau, 47, 61, 63
Teifi Valley Railway, 2
Tickets, iv, 27, 33, 38, 45, 47, 50, 54, 56, 57, 59, 60, 64, 73, 77, 78, 81, 83, 86, 89, 91, 105, 111, 122, 127
Trawsfynydd, 64
Tremadog (Tremadoc), 40
Twlldyndwr Level, 6
Tywyn
  Pendre, iii, 75-80
  Wharf, 11, 43, 73-75, 80, 81, 83, 87
Tywyn (Towyn), 11, 73, 74

Vale of Ffestiniog, 1, 56
Vale of Rheidol, 1, 110
Vale of Rheidol Railway, 1, 110-127

Wagons and vans
  brake, 9, 18, 30, 31, 55, 73, 74, 96, 101-103, 114
  cattle, 96, 107
  coal, 54, 69, 116, 117
  gunpowder, 19
  open, 5, 7, 9, 18, 19, 42, 65, 75, 76, 101-103, 116, 117
  tipper, 75, 84
Waterfall, 22, 29
Welsh Highland Railway, 1, 35-46, 50
Welshpool, 1, 96-98
Welshpool & Llanfair Light Railway, 1, 49, 50, 96-109
Whistling Curve, 59